Sebastiaan Kodden

BE A HERO

How To Bring Out Leadership In Everyone

Colophon

Be a HERO - How To Bring Out Leadership In Everyone
Sebastiaan Kodden
www.sebastiaankodden.com

Design and layout: Twin Media bv
Editors: Lilian Eefting, Leef in tekst, Groningen, the Netherlands
Publisher: BigBusinessPublishers, Donald Suidman
www.bbpublishers.nl/hero
ISBN: 9789491757525
First English edition: September 2017

Contents

Foreword

Foreword

The path I have taken in my private life and my career has been anything but predictable and standard. From lawyer to board member at an insurance company, from entrepreneur in recruitment services to executive coach. On this path, my motto has always been: "Make choices, live intensely, work hard." This motto has been an ideal constant for me, something to hold on to.

I see a lot of my attitude to life in this book by Bas about HEROes. This attitude – who do you want to be, being aware of that and taking control – determines to a large degree if you experience happiness and engagement in your life and work and achieve results. In this book, Bas explains really well what determines work engagement and whether you're using your given talents to achieve performance.

If you want to know how you can become more engaged in your life and your work, this book is a must-read for you! The book can help you look at yourself and your potential from a different perspective. As an executive coach, I therefore recommend this book to all the people I coach.

The book contains inspiring quotes and practical checklists that will activate your brain and stimulate your motivation. Its contents will automatically lead to valuable conversations about personal leadership and taking control. Only when you know which destination will mean success for you and your organization, will you know what path to take. The way will become clear, you will not take as many detours and you will spend less time going round in circles.

Each individual will choose their own valuable elements from the book, but I think it will help anyone who reads it to take the next step in their personal development. To become a person who does more, who is always aware of what and how they want to achieve and who takes responsibility for it. In short, a true HERO!

Petra van Trommel-Obèr LL.M, executive coach

Co-owner and director of: Success Group, executive coaching & consultancy, assessments and mediation Astorium, recruitment & secondment

Preface

Fifteen years' worth of entrepreneurship: it's done. Over thirty thousand hours of buckling down, of falling and getting back up. From living room to diverse other locations and everything in between. But also of fifteen years of study and research, eventually resulting in a PhD. What once started with the goal of improving my enterprise – after all, there is nothing so practical as a good theory (Lewin, 1951) – ended years later in a position at Nyenrode Business University, where I currently teach ambitious professionals in the field of leadership and personal development.

The question I suddenly asked myself during a break between classes hit me like a keeper who unexpectedly has to deal with a counter goal; what had I really learned during all those years of practice and study and which theory had I experienced as truly important? What was the real essence, why had certain things worked out well and others not at all in my practice? What had I enjoyed? And was the practice consistent with the various theories that I had gained over the years?

In his book *Outliers* (2008), bestselling American author Malcolm Gladwell underwrites the statement of Swedish psychologist Anders Ericsson (1996) that you can only arrive at successful insights after having conducted at least 10,000 hours of practice. In my case, these hours had been completed three times over – both in terms of practical experience and theoretical knowledge; it was high time to take stock.
Gladwell's book and Anders Ericsson's 10,000 hour concept provided a starting point for writing this book and for finding an answer to questions such as: which management theories have proven to be valuable during the past years? Which organization and management aspects actually lead to more work enjoyment, better performance and a higher chance of success? I hope to answer these questions, not only for myself, but for others as well.

In order to improve yourself, you must first have a vision and learn from mistakes made in the past, to subsequently continue your own development, as former hockey coach Tom van 't Hek once told me. To continue in line with Ericsson and Gladwell: 'Inspiration is great, but transpiration is better.' You will often encounter these key terms in this book: developing vision, determining your goal – the inspiration – but also booking the necessary hours – the transpiration.

Preface

Special thanks to my doctoral supervisor Prof. Dr. Rob Blomme – director of the Center for Leadership and Management Development at Nyenrode Business University – for his faith in me and the wonderful help and guidance during these past years. You are my example!
My warm thanks also goes out to all those who have dedicated their positive energy to this book, each in their own way. I would especially like to mention: Christel, my parents, my brother Berndt, Boudewijn, Edwin, Ineke, and many other family members and friends.
Finally, I would like to thank my heroes for the unforgettable encounters and their many quotes which I was able to use for this book.

Writing this book turned out to be an amazing journey. For all those who wish to read the book, whether despite or thanks to Confucius' words: 'It's better to travel one mile, than to read thousands of books", I hope that this journey with, and alongside, heroes will create a lot of positive energy.

Utrecht, September 2017
Sebastian Kodden

Introduction

Introduction

Heroes have always fascinated me: people who had accomplished something special or who seemed to be on their way to accomplishing something special. Those who did not seem to have any doubts and pursued their passion with positive energy. I loved to see their engaged attitude in life. As the son of a PE teacher, sports heroes especially had my attention. My heroes became my examples and many years later they formed the inspiration for this book, which I wrote with, and about, them.

I grew up in Raalte, Salland, a region in the east of The Netherlands, and spent my childhood mostly on the regional tennis courts. Thanks to my father's background, my brother and I were privileged enough to try out all types of sport and, in doing so, to discover our talents. Eventually, tennis turned out to be my greatest passion. I spent many happy hours playing, also to improve myself. I took my first job years later as a tennis teacher. In the end, my engagement for this job was too low. I realized that there had to be more to life than the local tennis courts. Unfortunately, my parents couldn't help me this time and I had to venture out on my own to find my path. When I was seventeen, I left for Groningen with the realization that I had no idea what I wanted to study and what I should be doing. The lack of focus was exhausting.

Years after completing law school with some difficulty, I studied Business Studies, once again in Groningen, which I enjoyed so much more. By then, I had become an entrepreneur and I realized that my legal background, knowledge, and managerial skills were not enough. During this new study program, I was handed many theories on leadership and personal development and I absorbed it all with great eagerness. These were my subjects, this was my passion...I was unstoppable! I handed over my enterprise to free myself up for my studies, this time at Nyenrode Business University.

In 2011, I received my PhD for research on the topic of engagement. After fifteen years of entrepreneurship, I still felt that, despite all my experience and studies, I still hadn't been able to put the finger on the sore spot and hadn't been able to answer the question; why do certain people and enterprises succeed while others don't? Until I came into contact with the concept and theory of engagement in 2009. Schaufeli & Bakker (2001), both connected to Utrecht University at the time, define engagement as 'a positive, affective-cognitive state of supreme satisfaction characterized by vitality, dedication, and absorption.'

I realized that these personal characteristics had made the difference for my childhood heroes, and not the fact that they had much more innate talent than the immediate competitors. It was also due to this engagement that I had achieved certain goals and failed to achieve others as an entrepreneur. Certain matters had been draining my energy, whilst I could hardly let other projects go because they kept pulling me in and forced me to complete them successfully. Vitality, dedication, and a capacity for absorption in your work are universal conditions for success. Your personal heroism is within reach if you pursue it with enough energy and engagement and don't give up before you've achieved your goals.

This book is about heroes and engagement. Or rather, a combination of the two. In this book, I've shaped the engaged person with the concept of the HERO: an acronym that stands for the 'Highly Energetic Responsible Operator'. HERO takes the theory of engagement as its basis and bridges the gap between (top-level) spots and management and personal leadership theories. As former PE teacher and current PhD in business, I noticed that many aspects of the engagement theory, which I had been researching for years, can be found equally in (top-level) sports. The aspects of vitality and dedication are, for example, vital to engagement: these aspects are also crucial for sporting achievements. For entrepreneurs, the same is true. The many similarities between engagement and sports were a reason for me to ask various Dutch sports heroes about their experiences with aspects such as vitality, dedication, and engagement.

'ENGAGEMENT IS A **POSITIVE STATE OF SUPREME SATISFACTION** THAT IS CHARACTERIZED BY VITALITY, DEDICATION, AND ABSORPTION.'

– Wilmar Schaufeli & Arnold Bakker

With practically applicable management theories, personal experiences, and encounters with highly engaged people, this book hands you a step-by-step plan to move from thought to action, allowing you to energetically take charge of your life. It is intended for anyone who is looking for new energy, passion, and engagement in their life. The book is also aimed at managers trying to make their organisations flourish by creating a positive flow.

HERO: 'HIGHLY ENERGETIC RESPONSIBLE OPERATOR'

The sources of inspiration and energy that heroes can be, form the central theme of this book. As a teacher at Nyenrode Business University, I teach the theory of engagement to young professionals, where I make ample use of practical examples gained within my own business. I tell them how important the various aspects of engagement have been, both within my own organization and to me personally, and the impact they had when things went wrong. I also address the reasons why the life lessons of a number of my heroes were so important to me and how they taught me to carry on and gain new energy. My students were the ones to encourage me to write this story down as a book.

I owe a great deal to my heroes. Not only for sharing their life stories and performances with me and for the energy they have given me to carry on, but also because some of them were willing to complete this book with me.

1
Engagement

B e *engaged, be happy,* as the theory of engagement teaches us. To feel that you are doing exactly that where your unique talents and interests lie and where you make optimal use of personal and work-related energy sources. Who does not want to be engaged? And which manager does not desire to have engaged employees? In tough times, engagement provides extra energy to cope with stressful situations, making these employees invaluable to the organisations they work in. However, studies into engagement show that almost 90 percent of the employees interviewed experience this work and life joy to a lesser extent, or not at all. In fact, many professionals indicated in my studies that they felt their engagement being drained because their talents were not appreciated and valued or due to the rigid company structure.

'88 PERCENT OF THE EMPLOYEES INTERVIEWED **ARE NOT ENGAGED.**'

Prof. dr. Arnold Bakker

What makes a person 'engaged' and which conditions allow him to perform optimally? To what extent should you display vitality and dedication to tap into that energy and passion every single day? And can engagement be learned/ taught and/or encouraged? These are all questions that could help us do the things we enjoy with more vitality and dedication, or to help us stop doing the things that only create stress and negative energy!

Vitality, dedication, and absorption

The theory of engagement (Schaufeli & Bakker, 2001; Bakker, 2010) posits that an engaged employee has a highly positive attitude that is characterized by an unparalleled zest for life, energy, the will to work, and to commit themselves fully. In the words of Schaufeli and Bakker: 'Engagement refers to a positive, affective-cognitive state of supreme satisfaction that is characterized by vitality, dedication, and absorption.'

1 Engagement

This allows the employee to achieve special performances. Those who are engaged, are open to new ideas, are both physically and mentally healthy, look for their authentic talents, and start every new (work)day with plenty of energy and a zest for life. This is not only pleasant for the individual themselves, but also inspiring for their immediate colleagues, and beneficial to the organization.

Therefore, the first step to becoming a HERO is the following:

Become a HERO– Step 1
Discover and develop your authentic talents.
Your zest for life and energy will increase significantly.

The state of supreme satisfaction is characterized by vitality, dedication, and absorption, three terms that may not immediately be clear. *Vitality* refers to the brimming of energy, feeling fit and strong, and being able to work inexhaustibly for long periods of time. *Dedication* refers to a high level of involvement in your work: the work is inspiring and evokes feelings of pride and enthusiasm. Finally, *absorption* refers to being absorbed in ones work, in a pleasant way, during which time stands still and it is hard to detach oneself from it.

I have completed various growth scenarios with my own enterprise, but I have also been forced to implement necessary reformations. I have provided leadership for many people, but I have also had to say goodbye to some of them. The double uniform of entrepreneur and leader, and that of shareholder and manager, has often created internal conflict. Later, I experienced that the eventual result always came down to engagement, both mine and that of my employees. Employees who demonstrated more or less engagement truly made the difference between success and failure.
The theory proved to be true, also for myself. To live is to learn and to learn is to live, as I have experienced.

Figure 1.1 presents the model of engagement and shows the means you need to become engaged. Sources of energy and task demands will be discussed separately in chapter 6.

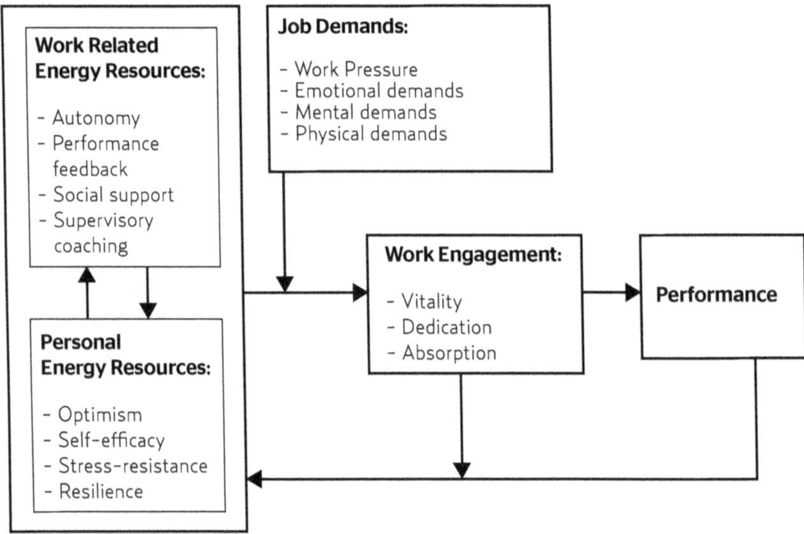

Figure 1.1: Model of engagement (Bakker, 2009)

Flow

People who are brimming with energy seem to find themselves in a flow, a concept that was elaborated on by American-Hungarian psychologist Mihaly Csikszentmihalyi. Csikszentmihalyi was one of the frontrunners of positive psychology and is the pioneer in the research into flow. Back in the 1970s, he researched people's 'optimal experiences', a state in which people find themselves when they are highly focused and experience intense enjoyment. I think that everyone has experienced such a state at least once: you do your work without any trouble, you feel strong, you feel in complete control of the situation, and you feel you are able to perform to the very best of your ability. Both the realization of time and possible problems vanish and you seem to be beside yourself completely. As if you are being carried by a fast river without having to swim.

Csikszentmihalyi discovered that people from a multitude of cultures, ages, and both sexes described pleasant experiences in similar ways. This gave rise to the first definition of flow: 'The state in which people are so involved in an activity that nothing else seems to matter; the experience itself is so enjoyable that people will do it even at great cost, for the sheer sake of doing it' (Csikszentmihalyi, 1989). In his pioneering work *Flow. Psychology of the optimal experience* (2007), Csikszentmihalyi describes how this pleasant experience can be reached, namely by setting goals for yourself and taking on challenges. By optimally aligning your knowledge and skills with the work requirements you demand of yourself (figure 1.2).

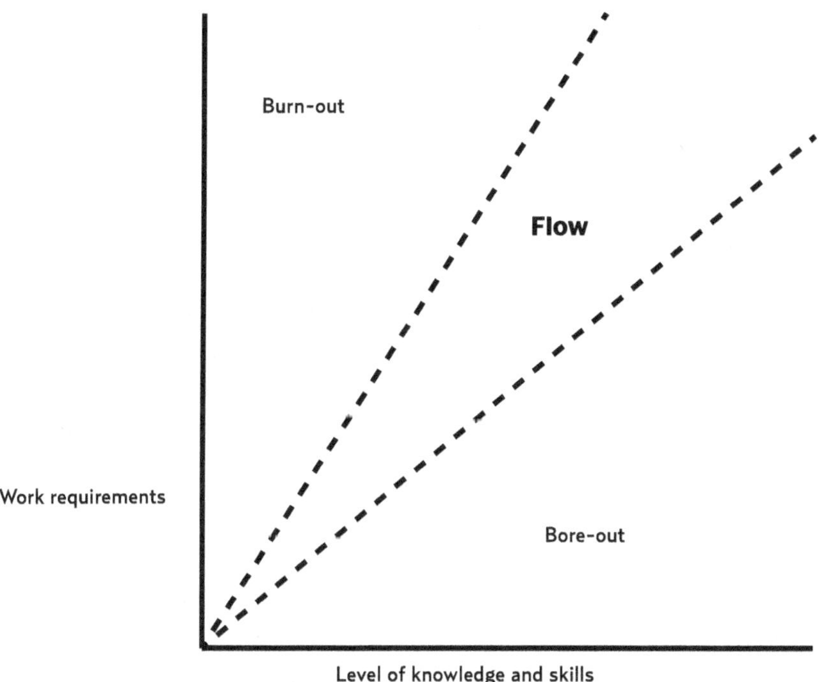

Figure 1.2: Flow (Csikszentmihalyi, 2007)

Research into flow at work shows that employees experience flow three times more often during work than during their spare time, whilst they actually feel happier in their spare time (Csikszentmihalyi & LeFevre, 1989; Rheinberg *et al.*,

2007). This is most likely due to the fact that we often use our spare time for activities that are not conductive to flow.

For example, Dutch people watched an average of fifteen hours of TV per week in 2006, whilst this is a passive, flow-inhibiting activity (Csikszentmihalyi & LeFevre, 1989). Following classes and studying do not lead to an optimal experience for most people either. Sport, on the other hand, is an activity that is most often reported when people were asked which activities create such a 'flow' zone (Rogatko, 2009). Passive activities generally have a negative effect on the experience of flow. Therefore, we can assume that a certain level of activity – physical or mental – is required to be able to experience flow. Dancers, mountaineers, puzzle enthusiasts; for them, the optimal experience is a recognizable feeling (Vleugel, 2011).

Flow is a state of being that leads to positive results for the individual and the organization. In my own research, I introduced a predictor that could advance or limit flow in a work context: namely, the organizational structures and especially the level of autonomy that is incorporated in certain organizational designs. During my professional career, I have experienced the way in which major law firms, and especially legal aid insurers, are designed as a hierarchic pyramid. The alpha male is in charge and the work for academically trained employees is protocolled so rigidly that autonomy hardly exists. The goal of my PhD research was to investigate the coherence between the work environment with regard to this level of autonomy and work-related flow experiences such as absorption, work enjoyment, and intrinsic motivation.

Engagement and flow show great similarities. However, an important difference is that flow is clearly situation-related (Fullagar & Kelloway, 2010) and can therefore change when the environment changes, whilst engagement is more consistent throughout time and displays characteristic-like properties. Or, in other words: engagement is an attitude that can be created and is not only a possible outcome of optimal circumstances. Anyone can become a HERO!

The next chapters describe the next steps for becoming a HERO: from discovering and developing your authentic talents in chapter 2, to the drafting of a masterplan for optimally using these unique talents in chapter 3.

2
Talent

ngagement is a life attitude that means that you try to use your talents and passions to the fullest extent with as much vitality, dedication, and absorption as possible. Former top swimmer and the Netherland's most engaged person, Erica Terpstra, once said the following on this subject: 'Try to color your life, push your boundaries, do something completely different if necessary. People tell me: easy for you to say, and they're right. I've always been lucky. I read something beautiful on this subject in a book on the Middle Ages. Two men are shaping rocks with small hammers. When they are asked why they're doing this, the one man says: "I chip rocks, and I will do so again tomorrow." The other man answers with a glint in his eyes: "I'm building a cathedral." That's the difference. In every profession and in every life, you can look for that special experience in the everyday.' (*Telegraaf*, October 16, 2012)
In my view, Erica Terpstra is right: the same talents can lead to entirely different results by adopting a positive life attitude and by utilizing talents better and with more energy. Merely having a talent is not a guarantee for success. There are plenty of examples of this in the sports world and in other areas. Think of media magnate Joop van den Ende, whom I greatly admire. Of course because of his achievements, which are unique, but also because of his life attitude. The entrepreneur tried his hand at practically everything before he developed his career as market leader in the field of large TV productions in the eighties. Van den Ende once trained as a carpenter and technical drawer. He tried to become a comedian and was the owner of a store selling party items for a while. This all failed. Until he discovered his talent: making others into stars. He developed this talent with a great deal of energy and passion. This made him into a hero for many. Although he is now over 65, he is not ready to retire, according to his business partner Hubert Deitmers: 'He continues to draw energy from new things, only now with even more focus.'

According to Esther Vergeer, one of the most successful Dutch athletes in history, that is where top entrepreneurs and top athletes are alike. Vergeer won gold in wheelchair tennis five times at the Paralympics. At the beginning of 2013, she gave up her sports career and made the change to entrepreneurship: 'The main similarities between top-level sports and entrepreneurship are working to the bone and having discipline. I think that it's important in both sports and entrepreneurship that you work according to a plan. You always have to ask yourself where you're going, what your goal is, and which steps you have to take to get there. Not being afraid to be innovating is also something that matches both athletes and entrepreneurs. This is often accompanied by taking risks.'

'THE MAIN SIMILARITIES
BETWEEN TOP-LEVEL SPORTS AND ENTREPRENEURSHIP ARE WORKING TO THE BONE AND DISCIPLINE.'

Esther Vergeer, Wheelchair tennis player

Utilizing your talents as a prerequisite

A nice quote from my PhD supervisor prof. dr. Lidewey van der Sluis is as follows: 'Everyone has a talent, but not everyone is a talent.' Talent is a combination of aptitude and preference. It is doing what you are good at (for instance organizing and negotiating), plus doing what you like (such as managing). Some talents clearly manifest themselves in our childhood, and others will only become visible later on. You develop your skills through your education and experience, for instance gained during your studies, volunteer work, sports associations, or your first job. You will have often already made subconscious choices to do just that for which you have a talent (even more).

It is a common misconception that skill is the same as talent (Covey, 2010). Talents do require skills, but people can have skills and knowledge of certain matters, while they still do not possess a talent in that field. If a person has a job that does require skills, but that does not tap into a person's talents, this will never give rise to engagement: the work has to be done, and you do possess the necessary skills, but are you really enjoying it...?

Step 2 of the step-by-step plan of Become a HERO is therefore as follows:

Become a HERO - Step 2
Draw up a masterplan and develop a final goal for
those topics that tap into your talents and passions.

In order to become a HERO, talent alone is not enough: you also have to be able
to utilize your talents to be effective and successful. To deliver unique rather
than average achievements. Therefore, your personality is just as important for
the development of your talents. Only those who act can become a HERO.
Prof. dr. Lidewey van der Sluis employs the 3C model. According to this model
(Van der Sluis, 2009), there are three elements that determine the talent profile
of an individual: character, capability, and capacity. *Character* constitutes the
core and says something about your motivators, your personality, and your ego.
Around this, we find the shell: *capability*. This comprises of your skills and
behavior. The outer shell is your *capacity*, your expertise, your track record. Van
der Sluis says the following: 'If you're lazy and lack discipline, it doesn't really
matter how much competence and knowledge you possess: you won't utilize it.
You will only learn what your development potential is, if you get to know yourself on all three points' (2009). Van der Sluis later added a fourth, an especially
important C: *climate*. Or the environment in which you work or learn. You can
possess all the talent in the world, but the context determines whether you are
able to become a talent.
I certainly recognize these findings by Van der Sluis, and they also applied to my
heroes. Whether it concerned Pieter van den Hoogenband, Erben Wennemars, or
Jacco Eltingh: they had all searched for their talents before they became heroes.

'TALENT IS NOT THE SAME AS
COMPETENCE, IT IS RATHER
A CONDITION TO PROPERLY
MASTER A COMPETENCE.'
– Prof. dr. Lidewey van der Sluis, Nyenrode Business University

---

Van der Sluis: 'Talent is not the same as a competence, it is rather a condition with which to properly master a competence. Take for instance the competence "achieving". We live in a world of show, so everything must be presented. There are those to whom this comes naturally. As they do it more often, they improve. Others simply don't have it. You can bring someone from a fail to a pass, but we shouldn't force them to excel. This won't make them any happier or more productive. It's better to develop someone's talent. If, as a tennis player, you've got a strong forehand, but a weak backhand, you're better served in putting your energy into improving your forehand. Research also backs this up. Work on the basis of the strength people naturally possess. Therein lies the power to develop. In doing so, the natural ability will actually be used and you will allow someone to become a talent based on the talent they possess' (Van der Sluis, 2011).

A competence to be acquired may come naturally to you, or it may not. You can have a talent for it. However, this talent is strongly dependent upon your personality, Van der Sluis posits. 'You can take a kind of picture of a person's personality profile. This allows you to discover to what extent these characteristics are present in someone's personality. By means of this picture, you can predict to what extent a person is suitable for a certain competence. The beauty of it is that you can translate various personality traits into competencies. "Collaborating", for instance, is related to extraversion and openness, the extent to which you assign importance to your environment and attune your environment to this. If you have high scores on these personality traits, you will sooner have the tendency to work together with others. If you are more introverted, you can learn to collaborate, but it doesn't come naturally to you. Because, deep down, you can't or don't really want to. You will never become a true team player. It is possible to develop personality traits, but this requires a lot of time and effort. In short: the roots of competence development lie in a natural given factor, namely your personality.'

According to Maurits van Rooijen, former rector magnificus of Nyenrode Business University, discovering and developing talents should not be viewed as voluntary. 'You have a responsibility towards yourself, your family, and your friends, towards your company and your colleagues, to develop these talents and to let your immediate environment share in your achievements and personal happiness. Everyone benefits from a happy person in his or her immediate environment, more so than from someone who continues to struggle and complain about missed opportunities in the past. So, do yourself and others a favor and accept this responsibility' (in: Nyenrode brochure Doctoraal Programma MSc, 2010).

'DISCOVERING AND DEVELOPING YOUR TALENTS SHOULD NOT BE VIEWED AS VOLUNTARY. EVERYONE BENEFITS FROM A HAPPY PERSON IN HIS OR HER IMMEDIATE ENVIRONMENT.'

– Prof. dr. Maurits van Rooijen, former rector magnificus Nyenrode Business University

---

The wish to discover your talents has nothing to do with ego, but everything to do with taking responsibility. After all, you can only be proud of developing your natural talents, the other things have simply come naturally to you. Talent is beginner's luck, in the words of Toon Gerbrands (2011). Buckingham (2006), says the following: 'Viewed in this way, neglecting your strong points and focusing on your weaknesses is not a sign of diligence and modesty at all. It even borders on irresponsible behavior. The most challenging and honorable mental attitude which demonstrates the most responsibility is to recognize potential strong points, that lie hidden in your talents, and to look for ways to realize these.'

You have to continue to reinvent yourself and to innovate to be able to possess the desired energy. Many of our talents will otherwise remain undiscovered and unused. The importance, but also the problem with this statement, is shown in a study in *Elsevier* (June 2012) among graduated academics: over 25 percent of the graduates regret the choice he or she made for their studies and would have preferred to study something else. An expensive mistake, that can be determinative for the rest of your life. Unless you have the will and perseverance to change the course of your life. For instance, by choosing another study that does suit your talents at a later point in life.

Research by Marcus Buckingham (2006), among others, shows that very few professional organizations work in a talent-oriented manner. If employees in American companies are asked during what percent of a normal workday they make use of their strengths, the answer is: 17 percent on average. In the UK, this number is even lower: 15 percent. Dutch employees have not been asked this question, but I do not have the illusion that they would score any better. It is as if you place a striker in a defense position running after his opponent during 80 minutes of the match. Only during corners is he allowed to come forward. The example may appear juvenile, but this is apparently the way in which many employers employ the talents present in their companies, with the subsequent consequences. Employees who perform their work reluctantly, appear to be a huge liability for the Dutch treasury. According to research conducted by advisory agency &Samhoud, this loss may amount to as much as 15 billion Euros annually for a small- or medium-sized company. Grumpy employees are more often ill, will not bring in as much money, and that in turn reduces tax income.

Dedication and perseverance

In the Netherlands, the reigning idea still seems to be that all success is only achieved with talent and that these innate gifts determine our future. In truth, reality is different. Although certain physical and mental properties, that is to say your talents, certainly can give you a head start, success is mainly achieved by practicing, practicing, and practicing some more. As Edwin van der Sar, Dutch goalkeeper, reported: 'The only thing that counts is hard work.' After his final match in the Amsterdam Arena, he was crowned the best and most talented keeper of all time. He did not want to comment on the first compliment, but he felt the second compliment was incorrect. Training hard, every single day, that had been the key to his success, as he said. The world famous pianist Vladimir Horowitz also once aptly expressed: 'If I skip one day of practice, I notice; if I skip two days, my wife notices; if I skip three days, the world notices.'

Another fine example is that of astronaut André Kuipers. Twan Huys interviewed him in his TV program *College Tour* and Kuipers proved to be a gifted speaker. Beautiful stories about viewing the earth from space, its vulnerability, and the adventure were alternated with anecdotes of his personal sacrifices to obtain that place on board of the spacecraft. Although Kuipers was nowhere near the most brilliant candidate during the selection rounds, his fascination and will to achieve his goals eventually gave him the edge and made it possible for him to realize his unique experiences: he already made two space journeys, of which the longest was approximately six months. When a student asked what Kuipers, following Neil Armstrong's quote upon landing on the moon, would want to tell humanity upon his first steps on Mars, Kuipers gave a stunningly simple, but striking answer: 'Never give up! If you have a passion, while the whole world feels this is complete nonsense and doomed to fail, you have to give it all you've got. And if you do fail, at least you know you've followed your passion and you will never be able to blame yourself for anything.' He himself showed ultimate dedication to achieving his goal and he succeeded.

'IF I SKIP ONE DAY OF PRACTICE, I NOTICE; IF I SKIP TWO DAYS, MY WIFE NOTICES; IF I SKIP THREE DAYS, **THE WORLD NOTICES.'**

– Vladimir Horowitz, world famous pianist

My own research into engagement and productivity led to the same conclusion: dedication made the real difference. As an entrepreneur, you learn not to walk around with your head in the clouds, but to keep both your feet firmly on the ground. But for the rest, I would fully agree with the revelations of this hero. Becoming an astronaut like André Kuipers takes courage. Courageous behavior is also a prerequisite for making unique achievements.

'NEVER GIVE UP! IF YOU HAVE A PASSION, WHILE THE WHOLE WORLD FEELS THIS IS COMPLETE NONSENSE AND DOOMED TO FAIL, YOU HAVE TO GIVE IT ALL YOU'VE GOT.'

— André Kuipers, astronaut

Engagement, energy, and perseverance have proved to be crucial talents for me to be able to survive as an entrepreneur and as a teacher. As a graduated tax specialist, I felt myself to be the worst in the Netherlands: no passion for the trade and a complete lack of ambition to excel. Let alone having a talent for it. Fortunately, I later found myself in the position of having to look for my talents. Currently, I am an engaged entrepreneur and lecturer in business. Although my faith in people has been damaged more than once and I did not always succeed, I have learned to handle these situations better and to persevere.

Erben Wennemars says: 'Having perseverance is also a talent.' He is completely right. That is also true for people like John de Mol, the largest media magnate in the Netherlands. He was a good soccer player, but he was not talented enough for a career as a professional player. He finished high school, but he seemed to be more talented for entrepreneurship and the media. When he was 23 years old he was already a freelance producer and he is now a billionaire. Of course, he sometimes failed, but this brought out the best in him. Think of the talent shows he was so successful in producing, with the ultimate crown on his work: the Emmy for TV program *The Voice* in 2013.

'HAVING **PERSEVERANCE** IS ALSO A TALENT.'

— Erben Wennemars, ice skater

Discovering your talents

It is now time to map your talents and to translate these choices and experiences into what you have learned from them and what aspects you have enjoyed. In this section, key questions will be discussed that can help you to discover your talents.

There is a top talent as well as a poor performer in everyone. According to the Management Development Agency MDI, our success or failure in a certain position or environment is largely determined by three factors:
• the **WHY:** our motivators, initially often hidden (which include our values, interests, and form the spectacles through which we view the world);
• the **WHAT:** our natural gifts and talents;
• the **HOW:** our behavior — both our natural behavior and the behavior we display in response to our environment (also referred to as masked behavior) (source: http://www.mdi.nl).

In his book *Discover your Strengths* (2006), Buckingham indicates how you can answer in particular the WHAT question. What are your talents? To find an answer to this question, Buckingham uses a handy acronym, SIGN:
• **S**uccess: you are good at certain matters and achieve results;
• **I**nsights: you anticipate on certain matters beforehand and feel you must do this;
• **G**rowth: these matters are relatively easy to you and you feel good doing so;
• **N**eeds: despite possible physical exhaustion afterwards, you feel great.

By being aware of these four signs, you can discover your strengths, according to Buckingham (2006). Buckingham shows that self-insight does not have to be so difficult: by holding up a clean mirror for yourself and by looking at yourself in a genuinely critical, but especially positive manner, you really do not need anyone other than yourself to bring out your unique talents. But, as we are social and vulnerable beings, we prefer to test our opinions in practice and in relation to others.

Within this framework, the hedgehog principle of Jim Collins (2001) can also be discussed: the hedgehog as a metaphor for the starting point that, as soon as you discover what you can excel in, as soon as you truly understand how you could make a living, and know deep down where your passion lies, you will be able to overcome all crises. Collins uses the story of the hedgehog, who is attacked daily by the clever, quick, cunning, and skilled fox: by simply employing his only weapon, his spines, the fox stood no chance against the hedgehog. Even though the hedgehog was slow, small, and not particularly intelligent, the fox could not beat the spines.

It is his way of indicating that not only exceptionally strong animals such as lions, leopards, and rhinos are successful, but that even small, slow, and seemingly vulnerable animals possess innate, unique talents that allow them to survive and win. That is, if these animals dare to employ their talents. 'Fight, flight, but never freeze.' By using his spines, the hedgehog fought back, forcing the cunning fox to give up.

The principle of the HERO concept is similar to the hedgehog principle of Collins and the SIGN acronym of Buckingham: as soon as you know what your talents are and manage to develop these, you will find that you will become even more engaged. Your zest for life will increase (even your life expectancy, according to the hedgehog principle of Collins), you will enjoy your work more and you will have far more energy to give all you've got in you.

If you wish to uncover your talents, your spontaneous reactions will form important indicators. Reactions under extreme stress form an explanation for people's performances (Buckingham, 2006). Some see the humor in certain extreme situations, while others have an almost compulsive tendency to take charge. In addition to the closed questions of SIGN, Buckingham provides three more indications you must take notice of in order to discover your talents:

- **1** What are my strongest desires?
- **2** In which fields do I have the capacity to learn fast?
- **3** What are my feelings of satisfaction?

Strong desires reveal the presence of a talent, especially when they occur early on in our lives. The capacity to learn is another indicator for talent. Sometimes, you simply do not recognize a talent, because the call of your talent has not yet made itself known. However, this may occur even later in life or due to another factor, for instance, by trying something new. Feelings of satisfaction form the last clue for having a talent. After all, it is quite obvious, when you feel comfortable doing a certain activity, you have made use of a talent: do what you like doing!

It is highly recommended to search for your talents thoroughly and maybe also with help from the people around you, but various websites, including www. finale.nl, also offer tests that help you map the why, what, and how. These tests must expressly be viewed as a tool. The results of such a test could indicate that you have a highly athletic nature, that you possess a strong sense of perseverance and willpower, and prefer to work alone. But only practice will show whether or not this will make you into a talented ice skater or swimmer! The Dutch peanut butter brand Calvé had a commercial featuring swimmer Pieter van den Hoogenband. In this commercial, little Pieter, who cannot play soccer to save his life and shows great indifference to the sport, spontaneously jumps into the nearby water-filled ditch after another football training to begin his first swimming competition. The message in this commercial is spot on: you do not have a talent for everything, even when you have won multiple Olympic medals. You have to do the things you do have a talent for and what you are passionate about. And you should not be afraid to change course, otherwise you risk missing out on your talents. Sports appear to be an excellent tool to filter your talents and to become fully familiar with your personal characteristics. Nobody is good at everything!

'EVEN SLOW AND SEEMINGLY VULNERABLE CREATURES, SUCH AS HEDGEHOGS, HAVE INNATE AND UNIQUE TALENTS, WHICH CAN MAKE THEM EXCEPTIONALLY STRONG.'

— Jim Collins, author

As the son of a PE teacher, sports were a natural and important energy source for me. My brother and I could try our hand at all types of sport and every birthday was celebrated in the gym. I turned out to have a passion for tennis, although it was a shame that I did not discover this sport until my fifteenth birthday. My brother followed my path and together we reached a lot of finals that sometimes ended well, and sometimes did not. He was just as talented in tennis as I was and nothing is as disastrous as losing a club championship to your little brother. When that happened, my self-esteem was severely dented. However, I never lost my pleasure in the game and I won various other finals.

Later, I was asked to teach tennis which gave me the opportunity to discover my talent and passion for teaching at the age of twenty. Both my father and mother worked in education, so I could have known it was there, but talent and passion are of course not passed on as simply as that. Fortunately, this was the case for me, as it turned out from my teaching evaluations. Interaction with people and offering help with progress gave me a lot of positive energy. For instance, because timid children realized during the tennis lessons that they too had a talent and suddenly dared to speak up.

Nowadays, I consider myself lucky to have such positive energy and to have experienced the things which I have accomplished, but there have been several moments in my life when I was not engaged or when I was tempted to give up. Deep in my heart, I knew that I had to change course to regain my happiness, or that I had to push on to restore my self-esteem. At those moments, I often thought about my sports heroes, and especially the way they handled loss. 'You must be able to lose to be able to win again,' as Erben Wennemars once said.

A fine tool which can be helpful in discovering your talents is also the Success Insights Instrument: a validated test that provides personal insights in order to come to greater personal effectiveness, more pleasure in work, and more success in your career. There are multiple tests available that may provide similar contributions.

Developing your talents

Discovering your talents is one thing, being able to develop them is another thing entirely. This actually also involves a journey of discovery. Imagine that you have discovered that you can do presentations in a passionate way and manage to fascinate and interest your audience: this does not mean that you will be able to do so for every topic. Buckingham (2006) states that you must discover both your desired work field and your role in order to fully employ your strengths.

A good salesman who does not believe in his products will be less energetic in achieving his results than colleagues who do fully support the products. An employee who fully believes in the usefulness of his field of work, but who fulfills a role within this field that does not match his strengths, will eventually become miserable: seeing other colleagues who are allowed to do what he would like to be doing.
In order to truly develop your talents (or those of others), you must not be afraid to walk other paths and actively search for new opportunities and chances. Actively searching means that you must dare to change your thought patterns and preferred behavior, but also your role and/or work field. Ask yourself the following questions, in doing so:

1. **Why** am I here on earth? What do I live for and what are my deepest aspirations? Who am I? What is my basic attitude? And do I act in accordance with my basic attitude?
2. **What** has been critical to my success until now and which compliments am I given? Which personal aspects make me unique? And which of these personal aspects are essential to realize my aspirations?
3. **Which** of my personal aspects should receive more explicit attention for me to experience personal happiness?
4. **How** (role) and where (work field) are my talents best used? Am I currently in an environment in which I can fully develop my unique personal aspects? And why/why not?

By asking yourself questions, you return to the core of your existence. Be honest in doing so, but not too modest: no one is perfect, while everyone has talents. In order to discover and develop your talents, you must offer yourself (or others) the opportunity to fulfill roles that may not seem to suit you at first. Do not be afraid to do things you have never done before, but that do appear to match your basic attitude.

Working together on talent

The statement of Van der Sluis that not everyone is a talent, is also true for Jacco Eltingh. A tennis player who managed to reach the top; winning Wimbledon – but only by working together and by utilizing his talents (better). As a single player, Eltingh achieved reasonable success, but he only made it to number nineteen in the world in 1995. As a double with Paul Haarhuis, however, he was far more successful. By retaining his engagement for the game and better use of his talents, Eltingh once again took charge of his tennis career and achieved great success. Together with Haarhuis, he became world champion twice (in 1993 and 1998) and they were the first team to win all four grand slam tournaments. The KNLTB (Koninklijke Nederlandse Lawn Tennis Bond, or *Royal Dutch Lawn Tennis Association*) appointed them as honorary members, and rightly so.

That collaboration can lead to better results is true for us all, and here only people with vitality and dedication can make the desired difference. Quality trumps quantity. In 2008, I spoke with the late Ronald Naar, the most famous mountaineer and expedition leader in the Netherlands, about selecting the right team members. 'Team members that possess skills you don't have yourself can help you best in achieving your goals. Don't be afraid to include capricious talents in your team. They are often the right people to help you to realize your goal.'
Top performances are achieved by means of a combination of amateur engagement and professional skill and ability, according to Naar. 'True victories are never easy. Top-level sports achievements are generally the result of a lot of training, both a thorough physical and mental preparation, and the discipline to continuously work on technical and tactical improvement. Talent alone will only get you so far, and usually not far enough. On the road to the top, indolence is your biggest enemy.' His book *Naar de top* (2007) beautifully describes how no one is that complete that he can reach the top on his own and that open and honest communication in a team are therefore so important. 'Selecting the ideal partner to accomplish extreme climbs successfully is an alpinist's most important, but also most challenging task.'
In 2011, Naar died doing what he was best at; during a climb of the Cho Oyu in Tibet. On the road to the top. The icon of Dutch mountaineering was honored for his perseverance, his efforts, and his significance for the sport. His brave choices and ultimate dedication did not only make him a great sportsman, his teambuilding and leadership insights are still used by many to achieve better performances.

In terms of discovering and developing talents in others, I consider Louis van Gaal the best Dutch example. Countless famous soccer players have made their debuts under his charge. In his first match as coach of the national soccer team, Van Gaal debuted no less than five players. And during his first term as selector for the national team, between 2000 and 2001, Van Gaal allowed fourteen players to debut.

'TALENT ALONE WILL ONLY GET YOU SO FAR, AND USUALLY NOT FAR ENOUGH. **ON THE ROAD TO THE TOP, INDOLENCE IS YOUR BIGGEST ENEMY.'**

– Ronald Naar, mountaineer and expedition leader

However, at the end of 2001, Van Gaal painfully became aware of the fact that talent development requires time, and is therefore perhaps better suited to the position of a club coach. As club coach of Barcelona, Van Gaal returned to the Netherlands in 2000 to prepare the national team for the world championship which would be played in South-Korea and Japan in 2002. The Dutch national soccer team failed to qualify for the world championship by losing to Ireland, despite achieving 20 points in a pool that included Ireland and Portugal. Given the average number of points per match, the Dutch team performed considerably better under Van Gaal's charge than it had in the preceding ten years, but the team still failed to qualify for the final tournament as it failed in the matches against direct competitors. Van Gaal was visibly annoyed by the attitude of his players and decided to quit on November 30, 2001. He was replaced by Dick Advocaat and he later returned to work as club coach at FC Barcelona. Van Gaal called the elimination in the world championship the greatest disappointment in his career as trainer.

> One day, before Van Gaal resigned, I met him in his office at the KNVB (the Royal Dutch Soccer Association). After having used soccer player René Eijkelkamp as the face of Finale for several years, I was looking for a new face for the development of a new website and style. And I thought, and still think: you have to look for the highest achievable option. A bet between colleagues got very out of hand, one employee asked: 'Why don't you just ask the national coach?' 'Okay, I will,' I replied, 'let's go for the highest possible option.' I didn't realize that this statement would immediately be used against me. I had no choice and the letter had to be written. I was already nervous when sending the letter. When I was called a week later with the announcement that Mr. van Gaal wished to speak to me personally, I nearly fell off my seat in surprise, and even more so from the shock. I went to Zeist ten days later, trembling. I already knew that the Dutch team had just failed to qualify for the World Championship, meaning that I probably wouldn't find Van Gaal in the best of moods. But when I saw all the cardboard boxes for moving house, I started to panic. How do I get out of here, I thought.
>
> Exactly one hour later, and without Van Gaal having blinked his eyes once, I got back in my car completely bewildered. We had agreed that Van Gaal would enlist the help of his advisers and would contact me by telephone two weeks later on a Wednesday afternoon at twelve pm to discuss a possible proposal.
>
> Exactly at that time and not a moment later, the phone rang. He immediately told me that he, with his advisers, had chosen a commercial of Albert Heijn (a supermarket chain). Within ten minutes, he explained exactly why and he had even had a full report of twenty pages drawn up which he would send to me. Which he did.

Van Gaal's professional attitude and punctuality are considered unparalleled by many. These skills, combined with a sense of talent development, accessibility, and interest in others, make him a true HERO. A true highly energetic responsible operator. To me, Van Gaal embodies the term HERO.

He also allows others to function as HEROes. One of the exercises that Louis van Gaal trains and repeats with his players, is to play in a different position than the player is used to. 'In doing so, left-wingers learn what it's like to be a right-back player. Which means that the striker has to defend. Understanding others, but especially being sensitive to what they experience is educational and eventually strengthens the collective and, consequently, the output. You can tap into people's ability if you know the space and scope people have. Unfortunately, this is often disregarded during the selection process. You have to base your selection on various roles: work magic with talents' (Van Gaal, 2009). Making talents into heroes, that is what it is all about. Our former and current national coach provided content for step 3 of the step-by-step plan.

'YOU MUST BASE YOUR SELECTION ON VARIOUS ROLES: WORK MAGIC WITH TALENTS.'

Louis van Gaal, national coach of the Dutch soccer team

Become a HERO – Step 3
Make sure that you enjoy the things you do and remain fully dedicated to your final goal.

Composing a team of engaged talents, who pursue a joint goal with full dedication and passion: this is not something that is only required in top-level sports to be able to win. The same principles apply in the corporate world and in science: within the right work climate, with the right people, who have the right, engaged work attitude, unique performances can be achieved. The next chapter discusses this topic: the importance of HEROes for every organization.

3
Heroes

Most people have heroes, or in any case people whom they admire. Some are not very taken to hero worship, but I have always enjoyed admiring people whom I greatly respected. Admiration for something they had achieved or accomplished, but often also admiration for the way in which they got there. I devour biographies that describe how dedication, perseverance and focus were essential for delivered achievements. Heroes serve as a role model: they can encourage you to push through when you are thinking of giving up. Heroes can serve as inspiration for pursuing goals that may seem impossible. Heroes have overcome obstacles that appeared to be unsurmountable. Heroes certainly do not have to be famous on screen: especially those people around us who have accomplished something or who have come through tough life phases with optimism, can be admired and can serve as an energy source.

HERO: 'HIGHLY ENERGETIC RESPONSIBLE OPERATOR'.

What is a HERO

Although the definition of engagement is rock solid, my thoughts continued to travel back to the link between top-level sports and energy. Consequently, I created my own definition of engaged persons one evening: that of the HERO. Also because I missed the aspect of utilizing talents in the definition of engagement. I felt that I was always engaged in my personal life, but I was unable to tap into my energy properly because I did not use my talents. When I took charge of my own life by changing course, I rediscovered my talents and my energy and only then did my performance really improve.

Since Einstein, we have known that energy is at the basis of all things. Without energy, there are no raw materials, there is no labor, and there are no end products. Energy is the very core of everything in the world around us. For the production of any item found in the store, energy is required. Energy, and preferably a lot of energy, must also be tapped into in order to achieve something. And you must act, not remain still. Therefore, I define my HERO as follows: *Highly Energetic Responsible Operator.*

The term HERO can also be described in a broader sense: the *highly energetic person, the engaged individual, who takes charge of his own life by optimally utilizing his talents, allowing him to accomplish unique achievements.*

The concept of HERO has been presented in figure 3. Not coincidentally has the definition of HERO been placed in a triangular model; I consider triangles to be the most powerful models available: not only are three points easy to remember, but triangles never fall over and each leg is as important as the other. A natural balance arises in triangles and maintaining balance is one of the most important things in life. Later I will discuss another beautiful triangle, that of the most important elements for good leadership: vision, meaningfulness, and authenticity.

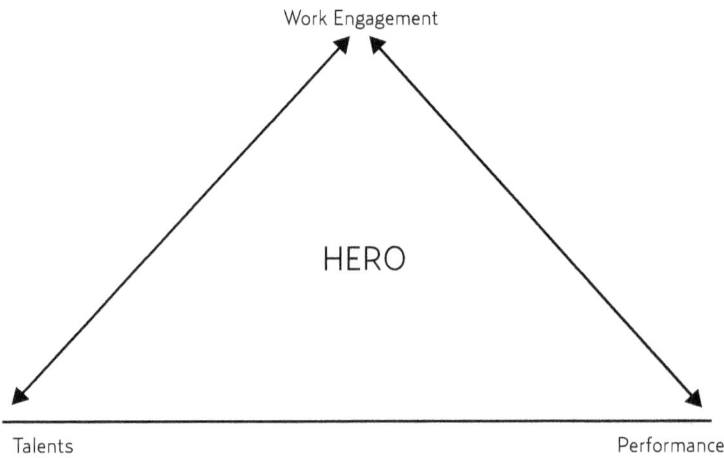

Figure 3.1: Model of HERO

I have sometimes jokingly referred to the counterpart of a HERO as a 'LOSER': the Listless, Obedient, Scared, Energy-draining Recipient (or worse; Shirker). These persons cost every employer money due to their unproductivity and their lack of energy. Or worse, they cost others, and their managers in particular, a huge amount of energy. 'Get the right people on the bus' is one of Jim Collins' most important tips. Ten years after the publication of *Good to Great* (2001), which according to many was the best business book of the past decade, he wrote *Great by Choice* (2011). In this book, he answers the following question: Why do some companies succeed in even the most chaotic and uncertain of circumstances and why do others fail to do so? Success, as Collins posits, is particularly a matter of making good and disciplined choices. One of the most important questions you must ask yourself is: do you still have the right people on board? Do they generate energy or do they cost energy? You can only become successful with heroes on board.

'GET THE **RIGHT PEOPLE** ON THE BUS.' — Jim Collins, author

A HERO has a master plan

Heroes are people who excel through courage or soul power, as the dictionary describes it. Heroes have a master plan allowing them to strive for their goals in an engaged manner, as one of my personal heroes, entrepreneur Joop van den Ende, told me. He recently spoke at Nyenrode Business University about constantly adjusting your personal master plan. 'You must have a master plan, passion, and a goal, otherwise you become rudderless. The world is at your feet, but that is also the difficulty. So, focus is essential,' he explained. It was music to my ears. His personal recommendation to young, ambitious students at Nyenrode Business University therefore makes up the fourth step in the step-by-step plan for becoming a HERO.

This had been the problem, I realized immediately: a master plan had been lacking completely until my 27th at least. An empty sheet of paper, that is how I would like to describe it now. After I had completed law school in 1995 with much difficulty, I found myself in the financial world with my specialization in fiscal law. First, at a major accountancy and tax consultancy firm, not much later as a newbie at a medium-sized financial consultancy firm. There too, I felt that I was not really using my energy and talents — should I have any — properly. The first time I had to show my talents, or rather, that my talents emerged due to the situation, was when my supervisor became seriously ill in 1996. Ruud Zebeda represented expertise, professionalism, and work engagement: every single day, he demanded everything of himself, and of others. I was confronted with his red pen strokes every day and as a fierce partner at the firm, he taught me not to choose the easy road. A message that is still valuable to me, even today. When he was suddenly no longer with us, after a short illness, he left a large void. But this also gave me room to discover my talents and shape my goals.

'HEROES: PEOPLE WHO EXCEL THROUGH COURAGE OR SOUL POWER.'

Van Dale / Encyclo

During Ruud's absence, I had taken over his role, also in providing inspiration, as none of the other, much older, team members wished to fulfil this role. They thought things were fine the way they were. Only when I had conducted research into engagement years later, I understood that I had been dealing with so-called satisfied but not engaged colleagues at the time. The level of activity was already low, became even lower and cost a tremendous amount of energy to raise. In the period that Ruud was ill, I thought we owed it to him to keep his department running until the moment he would return. Unfortunately that moment never came.

One man's meat is another man's poison is a terrible saying, but as is the case with many sayings, it is true. Because Ruud was suddenly gone, I discovered talents I did not know I had: perseverance, entrepreneurship, and the capacity to manage. These were talents I had not really needed until then, but they certainly came in handy.

After a while, Ruud's position had to be filled and the displeasure returned. My time was absorbed by many meetings and too many obstacles: I felt that I still was not using my talents to the full. I carefully started to think about my own passions, my authentic talents, and my personal goals. And this was very enjoyable to me. Making plans did not only appear to be great fun, but it also provided a lot of energy and inspiration to actually do something. As green as grass, I started on an adventure of entrepreneurship when I was 27: a financial temporary seconder who should make both people and organizations within the bank and insurance world grow. A journey that had many wonderful and less wonderful moments. Beforehand, my former director had warned me: 'Bas, beware. It all sounds fun, but entrepreneurship is hard work, hard work, and more hard work.' And he was perfectly right.

Every day again, we would make a difference, that was my dream. Not just by completing tasks, but especially by taking the initiative and showing responsibility. And by helping colleagues come into their own and get them moving. Because every journey of a thousand miles starts with a single, first step, in the words of Lao Tzu, who lived from 604 BC – 507 BC.

Until 2010, I led my own heroes full of passion. After twelve and a half years, I decided to hand over my enterprise so I could fully focus on an even greater passion: teaching young, talented managers and supervisors to be, conducting research, and writing management books. After a long journey, I had finally found my own destination.

The energy, dedication, and work engagement always remained and I experienced that working hard can certainly be fun. As is the case with running: it can be difficult the first few times, and you may come home feeling terrible, only to sit on the couch feeling great about yourself not much later. Entrepreneurship is like top-level sports, as they sometimes say. You have to lose a few times to be able to win. But both in entrepreneurship and in sports, you must first reach the finals before you can win or lose.

As a sports enthusiast, my heroes are mainly top athletes and coaches who do not only achieve special things, but have also left a special impression on me because of their attitude and appearance. Engaged people, who have walked their path energetically and performed unique deeds. Personal meetings with a few of my heroes have taught me more about themes such as energy, engagement, and (personal) leadership than years of study and research.

Take for instance Toon Gerbrands, director of soccer club AZ. He is both a top-level athlete, top coach and a director in company life. 'Talent is beginner's luck.

'AN ENTERPRISE POSSESSES A LIMITED CAPITAL AND A LIMITED AMOUNT OF MANAGEMENT TIME. **WINNING LEADERS INVEST WHERE THE RETURN IS HIGHEST!**

– Jack Welch, former CEO General Electrics

'TALENT IS BEGINNER'S LUCK,
YOU MUST SELECT ON MENTALITY.'

– Toon Gerbrands, director AZ

You must select on mentality. True top sportsmen possess talent, character, as well as intrinsic motivation.' I completely agreed. Both in the business world and in top-level sports, the same rule applies: eventually, it all comes down to vitality, dedication, and the engagement to achieve the desired goals.

Gerbrands subsequently stated a nice quote from world champion chess Bobby Fischer:

'I don't believe in psychology, I believe in making the right moves. You must act and not only think.' In other words; be a HERO: a highly energetic responsible operator.

It is not always just about winning

When, at the end of the nineties, I had just become a manager, I attended a seminar by someone who was viewed by many managers as a hero: Jack Welch. And although I admire him for his achievements – Jack Welch made General Electrics into one of the foremost and most successful enterprises in the world and was even made 'manager of the twentieth century' – he was not and is not my hero. Because Jack Welch only cared about winning. He even wrote a book about it, entitled *Winning*. He had a mentality that all CEOs of major companies sported in the nineties. Think of all the stories of Rijkman Groenink from ABN Amro and Cees van der Hoeven from Ahold, so brilliantly written down by Jeroen Smit. It did not matter how, as long as winning was assured. Strategy became more important than customers, and increasing the profit became more important than employees.

During the seminar in Amsterdam, Jack Welch taught about his strategy of differentiation. Not in products or services of GE, but in employees. According to him, enterprises can only win when the managers make a crystal clear distinction between employees performing in an optimal or substandard way, where they cultivate the strong and get rid of the weak. Winning leaders invest where the highest return lies. Managers within GE must evaluate each of their employees and divide them into three performance categories: the top (20 percent), the average (70 percent), and the group that displays substandard performance (10 percent). Subsequently, they were obligated to act accordingly: the 20 percent that performed optimally were rewarded with bonuses and option settlements, the 70 percent of average employees must be managed differently, and the bottom 10 percent – and he was very clear on this – only had one option: they had to go. The '20-70-10-rule' as the basis for winning might have worked for GE, but it made me feel terrible. That General Electric had to be saved from downfall later on by the Obama government, or the American tax payers, confirmed to me the illegitimacy of such a theory.

Winning is important, and so is return, but winning should never become so important that human beings are considered robots that must be replaced at the smallest glitch. Eventually, it comes down to whether or not a good match can be played again. It is harsh to have to conclude that Jack Welch's GE needed the money from the common people to do so.

It is clear: to me, it is not just about winning. And although I do consider winning to be the basis of being successful, I feel that the way in which this is achieved is equally important. My tennis heroes are above all Yannick Noah and Rafael Nadal. Although they never achieved the status of Pete Sampras or Roger Federer, they are still winners in my eyes. Noah only won one grand slam tournament in his entire tennis career and only reached a third position on the world ranking.

Federer and Sampras were perfectionists and stylists, but in many of the matches they almost appeared to be robots. Not a glimmer of emotion, being able to hit all the balls, and even victory was received with a simple handshake. I miss the energy, engagement, and passion that would bring me into rapture. Yannick Noah on the other hand, the Frenchman I believe was the first tennis player to return a lob ball to his opponent backwards through his legs, was brimming with engagement. His grimaces, his energy, his smash jumps, and the joy with which he played his matches: what a pleasure to watch.

I felt the same about Rafael Nadal a decade later: a modern gladiator who had exchanged his sword for a tennis racket. *El matador* as he is also called. Such force. He won a lot of matches, but he could also lose spectacularly, often to stylist Federer from Switzerland. Sometimes, you must lose in order to improve. Purely by analyzing his lost matches and by making better use of his talents, return, and backhand on grass, Nadal, the gravel specialist, even became champion at Wimbledon.

The feeling for the ball and high speed of Yannick Noah and Rafael Nadal and the many alterations in their strokes are talents that appeal to me far more than the twenty aces per match of Roger Federer and Pete Sampras. Nadal even returned to tennis in the beginning of 2013 with more energy and enjoyment after a severe injury and won tournament after tournament. As captain of the French team, Yannick Noah won the Davis Cup in 1991, for the first time in 59 years; a dream he realized in the final days of his career. Think back to step 1: being dedicated to your final goal is one of the conditions of becoming a HERO.

Engaged people are intrinsically motivated

Appreciation differs from giving rewards, I believe. Therefore, I disagree with the differentiation and motivation techniques of Jack Welch that state that the best employees must be rewarded with the highest bonuses and the most options. I assume that most professionals are intrinsically motivated to use their talents and are consciously working to get the best out of themselves and to make a contribution to their organizations. The manager who, just like the banks, thinks that winning is only about money, will be sorely disappointed.

Winning is more than playing a single match, where soccer players can simply be switched. Taking on and retaining engaged players and employees, that is what it is all about. Engaged employees are intrinsically motivated to perform, will exert greater effort than non-engaged employees, and remain connected to the goal and the enterprise longer.

Yet, most managers continue to believe that money forms the basis for a positive work relationship. Even managers who are active in the sports world: our celebrated Olympic athletes of 2012 received a check for their achievements: € 30,000 for a gold medal, € 20,000 for a silver medal, and € 10,000 for a bronze medal. I do not comment on the amount of money, but the gesture simply seems embarrassing to me. Not only towards the athletes who have achieved these extraordinary accomplishments, but also towards the Olympic idea that apparently had to be relinquished at the end of the tournament. Is an amount of money the value of winning at the Olympics? Millions of Dutch people had enjoyed it and many had even felt emotional, both upon the winnings and the losses. And this emotion was converted into Euros upon the athletes' homecoming. I do not believe that a single athlete had asked for it.

4
Energy and vitality

As discussed in chapter 3, my definition of a HERO is that of a highly energetic person — the engaged individual — who takes charge of his own life, by utilizing his talents to the full, giving him the opportunity to achieve unique performances. The following question is perhaps more interesting than who my heroes are: Why did they become my heroes? What made them so special? In all cases, it came down to the fact that I admired them for their positive attitude in life. Whether this concerned Erben Wennemars, Jacco Eltingh, Esther Vergeer, or Joop van den Ende: they all appeared to be brimming with energy and engagement. Mark Rutte once said the following: 'I know ageing thirty-year-olds and youthful seventy-year-olds. When minister Opstelten walks in — who would have been the oldest minister ever if we had started our first cabinet — the average age in the room actually decreases. Such an energy bomb, it's incredible.'

Research into engagement irrefutably shows that each organizational success can be traced back to the enthusiasm and passion of the employees. Engaged employees work harder and are more goal-oriented (Van Rhenen, 2008; Bakker, 2009; 2010; Kodden, 2011). Something organizations could use well in these times. Do more, with less people. A more shocking result from this series of studies into engagement is that 88 percent of the employees researched either do not or barely experience this work and life joy. It is not strange that the percentage of employees who are satisfied is higher, as I experienced later. Before I met prof. dr. Herman Kuipers in the summer of 2008, I was fully convinced that satisfied employees were crucial for the performances of organizations and especially knowledge organizations. I had written a business thesis and referred to various scientists who supported this idea — including David Maister of Harvard Business School.

Not satisfied, but engaged employees are crucial to every organization

In his book *Practice what you preach, what managers must do to create a High Achievement Culture* (2001), Maister discusses an empirical study into the relationship between employee characteristics, the quality of the relationship with the customer, and the financial end results. A statistically significant and causal connection was demonstrated. Just as Maister, I was convinced that employee satisfaction is crucial to the performance of knowledge organizations. It was not until later that I learned that Maister's employee characteristics went beyond mere satisfaction, but the penny didn't drop at the time. And it seemed so logical: without satisfied employees, there is no effort towards customers and a faster departure at the organizations they worked at. The annual studies of Great Place to Work also had satisfied employees as the starting point, which I thought was logical at the time.

Until I met Kuipers, who is now emeritus professor at the TU Eindhoven, who asked me scornfully: where have you been? Employee satisfaction deludes every superior and manager, he said. Still, many organizations conduct satisfaction studies among their employees to get an indication of their competitive position. They are used as a kind of thermometer to measure the health of their organization or to compare this to that of others (for instance Great Place to Work). The notion that satisfied employees will be more motivated to deliver good performances fuels this idea.

However, as soon as you take a closer look at the results from decades of research, it seems that employee satisfaction is hardly correlated to the degree of absence through illness, the level of personnel turnover, and the stress level. Whether you measure satisfaction in companies with a high or low level of absence through illness, much or little turnover, and a high or low level of stress; whether you conduct this study in companies with heavy labor conditions or not; whether you measure satisfaction in the one or the other country – employee satisfaction always approaches an average of approximately 70 to 80 percent (De Sitter *et al.*, 1997). The most likely explanation is that people tend to adapt to the circumstances in their organizations. They 'learn' to be satisfied with what they have. Viewed in this way, the employee satisfaction questionnaire is merely a weak indication of the quality of the work content and says nothing at all about future personnel turnover and the current effort for the organization.

These remarks from Kuipers opened my eyes: how often had I not asked an employee who was not functioning well whether he was still satisfied with his work and with me as a superior? I usually received the standard answer: 'Yes, very satisfied', while I felt no energy. While I received the answer: 'No, I am not satisfied. This, this, and this could be improved!' from other employees, who were performing great.

> 'There is nothing so practical as a good theory,' according to Lewin. The employee satisfaction questionnaire landed in the trash can immediately and was replaced by the engagement questionnaire.

Bakker goes even further by placing the term of employee engagement opposite to employee satisfaction. Satisfaction, as Bakker (2009) says, is an indication of employees who do enjoy their work, but have a low degree of activation. Engaged employees, on the other hand, also enjoy their work, but are additionally highly activated and motivated to perform their work. These are people involved in the organization who are also in a positive state of utmost satisfaction, that is characterized by vitality, dedication and absorption.
Satisfied employees deliver average performances, so it seems, while engaged employees, our heroes, are capable of delivering unique achievements for organizations.

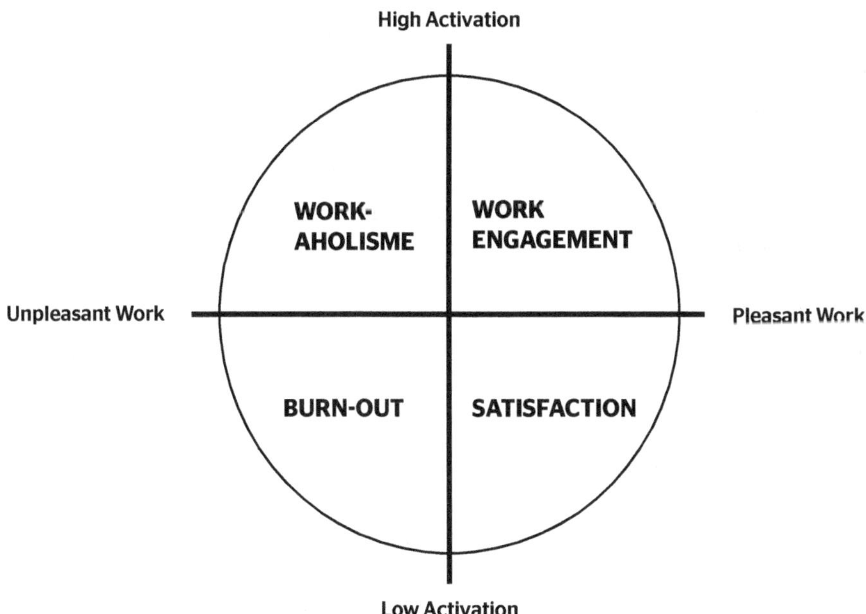

Figure 4.1: Types of employees (Bakker, 2009)

Working with engagement is not only important to the individual employee, but also for the employer. Engaged employees are more productive, more customer-friendly, loyal to the organization, and cause fewer accidents and make fewer mistakes. An organization simply makes more money with engaged employees (Schaufeli, 2001). Research by Bakker e.a. (2004), for example, showed that engaged employees receive higher evaluations from their colleagues: engaged employees are happy to do what they are asked and are more willing to help their colleagues. Salanova and her colleagues demonstrated that engagement has predictive value for the service-mindedness of employees (Salanova *et al.*, 2005). The results of a study among Dutch stewardesses (Xanthopoulou *et al.*, 2008a) were also very clear: engaged stewardesses were much more service-oriented than non-engaged stewardesses were. And restaurants in Greece achieved higher turnover on the days the staff were highly engaged (Xanthopoulou *et al.*, 2008b).

Between 2008 and 2010, I conducted research into engagement among Dutch professionals within the business service sector (Kodden, 2011). This study also confirmed the relationship between engagement and performance. Engaged professionals appeared to display more voluntary, extra effort than non-engaged employees and engaged employees appeared to be less keen to trade in their employer for another. The quality of the work and the employees' capacity to advertise the unique selling points of the employer to customers correlated to the level of engagement as well. The most important predictor for the achieved performances appeared to be the level of dedication of professionals, as an element of their engagement. In accordance with the definition of Bakker (2009), dedication concerns a strong work involvement: work is experienced as inspiring and evokes feelings of pride and enthusiasm.

According to the model of engagement (see chapter 1), employee engagement is fed by two types of energy sources:
1. **Work-related energy sources:** energy sources the employer is responsible for.
2. **Personal energy sources:** energy sources you youself are responsible for.

Both energy sources reinforce each other: an employee who possesses strong personal energy sources will also be able to receive more work-related energy sources. How the various aspects of these two types correlate and which energy sources we must have at our disposal in order to become engaged, will be elaborated upon in the following sections.

Engagement and work-related energy sources

Although engagement appears to be personal (you either have a positive life attitude or you do not), multiple studies indicate that work-related energy sources do positively influence engagement (Schaufeli & Salanova, 2002; Xanthopoulou, Bakker, Heuven, Demerouti & Schaufeli, 2008). Work-related energy sources concern the physical, social, or organizational aspects of the work. These energy sources are intrinsically motivating when basic needs are fulfilled, such as the need for autonomy, good feedback, and social support.
In my own study among Dutch professionals, I strived to explain the phenomenon of employee engagement from a structure and leadership perspective. My conclusion was that not only are engaged employees of vital importance to organizations, but also that leadership style influences this engagement. Earlier research had already shown that work-related energy sources positively correlated to engagement (Bakker, 2009). The manager plays an important role as formal superior, especially in making available work-related sources such as autonomy, social support, and feedback (Schaufeli & Salanova, 2002; Xanthopoulou e.a., 2008a and b). After all, superiors bear main responsibility for the amount of autonomy an employee receives, they must ensure feedback on the delivered work, and they are the ones who, partly, determine the amount of social support an employee experiences in his work.
Xanthopoulou e.a. (2008a and b), for instance, indicate that there is a direct, positive relationship between daily coaching (a work-related energy resource) and the daily engagement of employees. In chapter 8, I will discuss the new role a leader could fulfill in order to provide these work-related energy sources in more detail.

Engagement and personal energy sources

Engaged employees have much vitality and direct their own lives full of self-confidence (Bakker, 2009), and they create a lot of value for their employers. Not only for their employers: engaged people more easily change jobs if they are not challenged and/or create their own positive feedback by adopting a positive attitude and high action radius. Engaged individuals are able to overcome their fears and to take the next step towards their final goals.

Longitudinal studies show that once people are engaged, they remain engaged (Bakker, 2009). This is a conclusion that is very valuable in the pursuit of this positive state of being. People with more personal energy sources – that is, energy sources you yourself are responsible for, such as optimism, self-esteem, stress resilience, and personal effectiveness — appear to be better able to guard their own interests and remain intrinsically motivated for a longer period of time (Judge e.a., 2004). They pursue their goals because those goals match their personal interests and ideas and not because others feel they must pursue these goals. In 2003, Rothmann and Storm discovered a positive relationship between personal energy sources and engagement in police officers: they appeared to have an active coping style. They were problem-oriented and actively undertook steps to remove stress factors and remain engaged.

> An important different result was found by Xanthopoulou (et al., 2008): her team of scientists showed that personal energy sources have a mutual relationship with work-related energy sources. As the employees were more engaged, they appeared to have more work-related energy sources at their disposal and vice versa. Energy sources such as autonomy, coaching, and team ambiance were enforceable through optimism and positive energy.

Engagement is infectious

The infectiousness of engagement does not seem to be limited to colleagues at work; others appear to be positively infected by enthusiasm too. Recent studies show that employees even influence their partners at home with their enthusiasm (Westman *et al.*, 2011). Not only research, but also practice shows that engagement contributes to our psychological and physical health and vice versa, Erben Wennemars and I concluded after a joint reading. His practical lessons and the theory of engagement proved to match each other seamlessly.

> Notes from a joint reading with Erben Wennemars (www.han.nl), written down by employees of Hogeschool Arnhem Nijmegen
>
> August 31, 2012 - The name change of the Human Resource Management (HRM) study program, connected to the Faculty of Economics and Management FEM) of Hogeschool of Arnhem and Nijmegen (HAN) was the reason for a congress with renowned speakers. 'Engagement' is the theme for the success of the study program of the HAN, both now and in the future, as HRMer in the work field.

HERO-es

'Throw out all satisfaction surveys!' Bas Kodden, connected as program manager to Nyenrode Business University, started his masterclass with this statement. Satisfied employees and satisfied students are no guarantee for a golden future. As an organization, you must invest in engagement. Engaged employees and engaged students demand a different leadership style and a different educational method.

Give them space!

Give the engaged employee space to perform his project, task, or assignment. Let him choose his way and address his professionalism. But do make agreements and make sure these agreements are leading. In doing so, you allow your employees and students to become HEROes. In this context, HERO stands for highly energetic responsible operators, according to Bas Kodden.

Follow your passion

Erben Wennemars is the embodiment of the internal passion. Ice skating fast was always one of his passions, he was good at it. He achieved HERO status by winning titles and medals in ice skating. 'This was certainly not achieved without any hardships and setbacks,' Erban says. But by always following your passion, by believing in yourself and by working yourself to the bone and performing, you can reach your goals.

Now, after his active ice skating career, he must consider his life again. The world outside the races is a new challenge for Erban. With his emotion and drive as starting point, he wants to transfer his experiences to others. He would like to give youngsters a chance to become top-level athletes and is working on this idea for 'Erben's natural ice'. He teaches masterclasses to inspire adults and help them find the way to 'a golden future'.

(Source: http://www.han.nl/gebied/economie-management-recht/nieuws/nieuws/ helden-en-hrmers- een-goud/)

Engagement, dedication, energy and passion appear to be sources of success for many sports heroes. But as I discussed in previous chapters: success is relative. Your success or failure could be over by tomorrow and the day after tomorrow could offer new opportunities. By staying sharp — keep your saw sharp, as

---

'ESPECIALLY CHILDREN BECOME SMARTER FROM **DOING SPORTS AND PLAYING OUTSIDE.'**

— Prof. dr. Jaap Seidell, VU Amsterdam

---

management guru Stephen Covey puts it — and remaining fit, both mentally and physically, you will manage to utilize those opportunities. The importance of vitality exceeds that of booking one-time success: you are able to enforce happiness and wellbeing.

The importance of sports for happiness and wellbeing

Vitality is not coincidentally an element of engagement, in addition to dedication and absorption. Becoming a HERO requires vitality: a high level of energy to enable you to take action and to achieve your goals. And these goals do not have to be physical in nature (for instance, running 6 miles in 45 minutes). Vitality also improves your mental wellbeing. Vital organizations are carried by vital people. But how can you make sure that you remain vital?

In the United States, sports — American football, baseball, basketball, and ice hockey in particular — has formed a triangle with science and the business world for decades. Society profits from sports and vice versa. Especially the interwovenness with the college and educational structure results in the fact that smart minds are working on the development of those national sports, also without being asked (Van Breukelen, 2011).
Research from University of South Carolina shows that running, rowing, and other sports that make you sweat will not only improve your stamina, but are also beneficial for the brain. Going running for half an hour three to four times a week is enough to slow down brain degradation and even Alzheimer's in its early stages. Higher marks, fewer mistakes, better mathematical skills, forgetting less: (intensive) exercise makes you physically fit, but it also keeps your

'THERE IS A DIRECT, POSITIVE RELATIONSHIP BETWEEN MAKING WORK-RELATED ENERGY SOURCES AVAILABLE **AND THE ENGAGEMENT OF EMPLOYEES!**

– Prof. dr. Wilmar Schaufeli, professor

brain young (Nature Review, 2008). By exercising, you do not only stimulate your mind, but also your brain.

Especially children, who are developing all the time, become smarter when doing sports and playing outside. Particularly if this requires focus, communication, and coordination, according to Jaap Seidell, professor at VU University Amsterdam. 'It really concerns the step from doing nothing, to half an hour of moderately intensive exercise per day. That is where the greatest gain can be found.' Seidell realizes that many people who work hard all day are not very keen to exercise. 'But if those people take a walk or walk the dog, they will be much happier when they return. It's important to learn this early on. If you haven't done so your entire life and you are overweight, your knees are bothering you or you are short of breath, taking up exercise is a huge threshold to get over. That's why it's so important to remain active, from early childhood until old age.' (BNR)

Apply focus to remain energetic and vital

In order to become and remain vital, you must exercise, as many will tell you. But according to Tony Schwartz, founder and CEO of The Energy Project and author in the *Harvard Business Review*, the key cannot only be found in exercising, but also in managing time and energy. You must apply focus to live vitally — while our current *zeitgeist* forces one to multitask. Working, raising children, maintaining a social life, and exercising while you are at it. And preferably all in one day.

In his article 'The Magic of Doing One Thing at a Time', Schwarz indicates that we must limit ourselves to doing one thing at a time and must refrain from multitasking:
Why is it that between 25 and 50 per cent of people report feeling overwhelmed or burned out at work? It's not just the number of hours we're working, but also the fact that we spend too many continuous hours juggling too many things at the same time.
What we've lost, above all, are stopping points, finish lines and boundaries. Technology has blurred them beyond recognition. Wherever we go, our work follows us, on our digital devices, ever insistent and intrusive. It's like an itch we can't resist scratching, even though scratching invariably makes it worse. The

*biggest cost is to your productivity. In part, that's a simple consequence of split-
ting your attention, so that you're partially engaged in multiple activities but
rarely fully engaged in a particular one. In part, it's because when you switch
away from a primary task to do something else, you're increasing the time it
takes to finish that task by an average of 25 per cent.*
*But most insidiously, it's because if you're always doing something, you're
relentlessly burning down your available reservoir of energy over the course of
each day, so you have less available energy with every passing hour.*

Schwartz introduced energy management: making sure that you use your
energy correctly and maintain your energy. This advances your vitality. In a
movie clip shown during a presentation at Google, he shows a graph with two
lines: the capacity to perform on one line, and the demands set to employees on
the other line. The older the employee, the further apart the lines are. 'From the
day you are born, the capacity to perform increases without you having to do
anything for it,' Schwartz says. 'At what age do you think you've reached the
peak?' The Google twenty-somethings have no idea. Forty-five perhaps? The
energetic fifty-year-old Schwartz is visibly pleased by shocking the audience
with his answer: 'It's thirty! If you don't act, your productivity decreases from
your thirtieth. And that while the demands which organizations set continue to
increase. Houston, we've got a problem' (source: Intermediair, 2010).
Remaining vital has everything to do with applying focus. In his study, Schwartz
shows that the productivity of individual employees decreases with approximately 25 percent by performing different tasks simultaneously. Accordingly,
various other studies have demonstrated that multitasking does not work and
is even counterproductive (*Harvard Business Review*, 2012).

Remaining vital is crucial, in particular after your thirtieth, as research shows
(Machenbach, 2010). By exercising, but also by resting. And the latter is especially true for ambitious people, who produce more stress hormones than average and therefore need more time to unwind. If your body produces the stress
hormone cortisol for a longer period of time, this has a negative impact on your
immune system. A short break stops the production of cortisol and exercise will
even lead to the production of the happiness hormone endorphin. As Erben
Wennemars states: 'You must first disturb, then recover, in order to grow.
There's a reason why top athletes sleep as much as they do in order to remain
vital.'

The ancient philosophers such as Plato and Cleanthes also emphasized the importance of physical exercise. Plato, for instance, was a wrestler, Cleanthes an enthusiastic boxer. According to these ancient thinkers, self-knowledge and training – in particular physical training – play a very important role in your general vitality (Evans, 2012).

Only by staying fit can you achieve your final goal. The fifth step in the step-by-step plan is therefore the following:

> **Become a HERO – Step 4**
> Once you are physically and mentally fit, you can access new energy.
> Stick to your master plan, but be open to new ideas.

Burn-out: prevent energy loss

The number of Dutch people who suffer from stress or burn-out is rising rapidly. Most have no idea what the process was that preceded this, but the moment it went wrong is seared into the brains of many people who have had a burn-out. 'System coming down,' as a 53-year-old manager describes in a management magazine his physical and mental crash during a business trip to Singapore and Sydney. Burn-out also appears to be a sensitive subject, or even a taboo subject.

These past years, many publications have appeared on burn-out. Psychiatrists, doctors, psychologists, therapists, researchers, advisors, and experience experts have shone their light on the subject. The best book I know is one by Frank Schaper: *Geen tijd voor burn-out (No time for burn-out)*. A book that is also partly about one of my heroes: Joop van den Ende. In this book, Schaper makes a connection between character, life phase, and stress. Van den Ende speaks openly of his period of absence and illness. Two years after his burn-out Van den Ende had largely recovered. Often enough, he feared he would never recover at all. 'I really was in the wrong corner. I won my own Olympics.' He was already not feeling well a year and a half before his burn-out. A short temper, irritated more quickly. Lots of arguments, 'everywhere, with everyone'. At home, there was some level of understanding for it. 'But this is of course not done in a stock-listed company.'

His wife did point it out to him, and John de Mol also regularly advised him to look after himself. 'When I came home at night, I had to drag myself up the stairs. So tired, so broken. Workdays of sixteen, eighteen hours, seven days a week. And always that pressure, that responsibility. Because it had to be finished. After all, I'd promised. To my employees, to the stock market, to myself. And very gradually, the ground starts slipping from under your feet. You start to doubt yourself, your decisions' (*VN*, 2001). Van den Ende changed his attitude, said goodbye to energy-consuming projects, and took his health seriously, for the first time. He had to.

Not only top managers can suffer from a burn-out, it is also rather common lower on the career ladder. The *Nationale Enquête Arbeidsomstandigheden 2010* (NEA, in English *National Questionnaire Labor Conditions*), a study that is conducted annually by TNO and the CBS (Central Bureau of Statistics), it appears that a third of the working population at one point suffered from symptoms that were related to burn-out, where energy loss is the most noticeable one. According to research conducted by the CBS, complaints are so severe in approximately 13 percent of Dutch employees that one could speak of a burn-out. And this number seems to be growing: in 2007, this was only 11 percent. But this is not because we started working so much harder. On the contrary. Research by TNO shows that work pressure has remained relatively equal. The lack of both work-related energy sources (due to the crisis, managers increase control and decrease the employees' autonomy, for instance) and personal energy sources (the fear of being fired, for instance, tempers optimism) is the main culprit. Additionally, many people view tension- or stress-related complaints as personal failures and for that reason do not deal with them on time. Schaufeli: 'Complaints are often denied in the beginning. People often think: "It's part of it. I can take it." While they don't realize until later that these were the first signs of a burn-out. And that's a shame, because research shows that, once you have serious burn-out complaints, it takes two and a half years on average before you have completely recovered' (Schaufeli & Taris, 2005).

According to Schaufeli, you only run the risk when you put a lot of energy in your work, but feel that you do not receive much in return. It is not so much a question of the task demands being high, but that the energy sources are no longer available. I feel that this statement is perfectly true. The only time I felt less engaged myself were the moments that things were going well. Difficult times actually brought out a lot of energy in me. Apparently, I had a lot of personal energy

> sources at my disposal: optimism, self-esteem, and stress-resistance become
> more important in times of adversity. Work-related energy sources such as social
> support and autonomy also become more important when you are confronted
> with high task demands, such as high mental strain (Bakker & Demerouti, 2009). I
> certainly feel that I have had to deal with my share of mental strain during fifteen
> years of entrepreneurship, but this did not make me depressed. On the contrary.
> Only the lack of work-related energy sources has sometimes made me stumble.

Research shows that burn-out occurs more often among highly educated people
than among workers with a lower level of education. Additionally, burn-out
appears to be correlated to certain personal characteristics. The prejudice that
especially lazy and weak people suffer from burn-out because they are not able
to handle their tasks, is incorrect. It usually concerns, as is the case for Joop van
den Ende, particularly those people who have a high work ethic. They can work
hard for years, give their all and be flexible to do the work right and perform
optimally before they are felled. They fight until they drop, like marathon run-
ners who break down only after the finish and immediately start training again
for the next marathon.
You prevent a burn-out by living and working engaged, according to Van
Rhenen. And by making sure that you gain energy during your work rather than
losing it (Van Rhenen, 2008). The most important advice that specialized professionals give to avoid a burn-out: prevent energy loss, do not multitask (too
much), only do the things that are meaningful to you, and exercise; this will all
provide energy and make you stronger rather than weaker.

If work costs more energy than it provides, things go the wrong way. Luuk
Dewulf wrote about this in his book: *Help! Mijn batterijen lopen leeg (Help! My
batteries are draining)* (2012). As soon as energy sources are unavailable for a
long period of time, complaints such as being tired, sleeping badly, worrying,
and concentration problems will slowly start to arise which could develop into a
real burn-out.

More reasons to exercise

1. By exercising, your body is better able to draw oxygen from the air and transport this to your muscles. Per year, you lose 1 percent of this capacity. That results in a lot of huffing and puffing after the age of thirty. By exercising, you can half this effect.
2. Exercise lowers your blood pressure by preventing the clogging up of arteries.
3. By exercising regularly, your body is better able to break down glucose. This reduces the chance of diabetes type 2.
4. Exercise maintains your immune system and in doing so prevents aging.
5. Exercising breaks down your bodily fat. Moreover, the muscles you build will ensure faster fat burning, even when you are sitting still.
6. It keeps your bones strong. Our bones become 1 percent more brittle and thinner every year. By lifting weights for at least one hour a week, your bones will become stronger.
7. Exercising strengthens the muscles.
8. Especially stretching sports such as yoga or tai chi prevent arthritis.
9. When we exercise, we sleep better. Active during the day, tired at night.
10. It makes us happy. When exercising, we produce endorphins which reduces the chance of depressions.
11. Endorphins also make us less anxious.
12. By exercising regularly, you will be ill and absent from work less often.
13. Exercising improves the memory.
14. Exercising reduces the chance of developing Alzheimer's.
15. But most importantly: exercise gives you more energy. You will be less tired and less stressed.

Source: Psychology Today

It is clear that being and remaining physically vital is very important, I hope. But mental fitness is equally crucial for becoming a HERO. In the next chapter, I will discuss which energy sources are available to us, to a greater or lesser extent, to not only become vital, but also to remain dedicated to our master plan: to become a real HERO.

5
Energy sources for heroism

n the previous chapters, I have described how important HEROes, engaged
employees, are for companies. The chapters describe the importance of
work-related energy sources within the organization and also how satisfying it
is when you manage to utilize your own energy sources. Let's begin by visually
representing the model of engagement again:

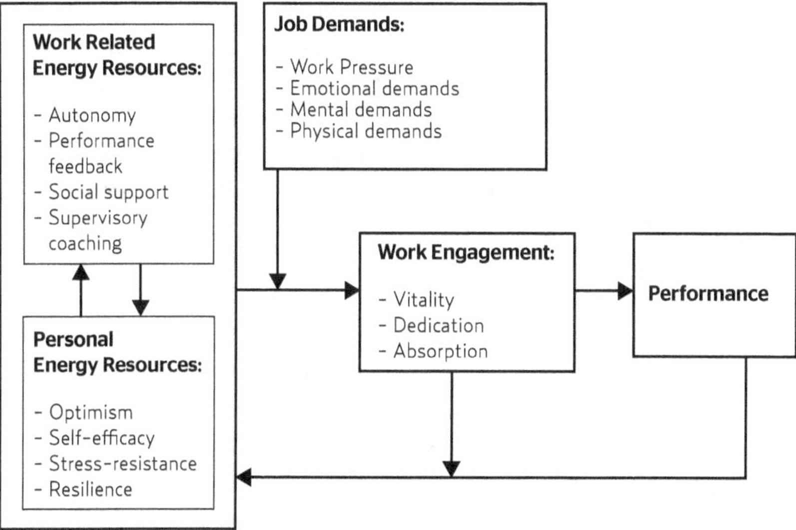

Figure 5.1: Model of engagement (Bakker, 2009)

In short, this figure shows that performances within organizations are dependent upon the engagement of employees, which in turn is dependent upon the
number of work-related and personal energy sources that are available to them.
These energy sources are discussed in this chapter: autonomy, feedback, social
support, coaching, optimism, self-esteem, stress-resilience, and personal
effectiveness. When discussing these energy sources, I will use a few of my
personal heroes as metaphors. Subsequently, I will also elaborate on the importance of high task demands for the relationship between energy sources and
engagement.

1. Autonomy

Geef ze de ruimte! (Give them space!) This is the title of the book by René Tissen, professor at Nyenrode Business University. In order to function properly, people need space in organizations. That sounds self-evident, but it is not. Because people usually do not receive the space they need, and the space they do receive often does not matter.

Tissen describes both the theory and the practice of spatial organizing. He shows how physical space (time and place), virtual space (working with digital technology), and mental space (experience) can be organized in such a way that employees can continuously improve performing the mission which the organization stands for and also in different ways if necessary. This can be done in a natural way that suits them. Top-down management becomes redundant because of his book, because people can and actually want to organize themselves. *Geef ze de ruimte!* Is an inspiring book for managers and employees who want to perform better and want to offer, take, and receive the space to do so.

The importance of autonomy was also demonstrated in my own study into employee engagement. It is no secret that legal professionals make long days, that the work pressure is often experienced as straining, especially by young lawyers, and that the call for autonomy rings ever louder. The question I asked myself was as follows: how can law firms keep their employees dedicated and productive nowadays and reduce the risk of the best people leaving the organization with all their knowledge?

Many policymakers within the legal sector grew up with the idea that scale increase leads to lower costs. This is understandable, as this was the case for hundreds of years. In agricultural economics as well as in industrial economics, scale advantages were needed at the beginning of the last century for low cost production and to maintain a competitive position. In the modern services economy, this relationship no longer holds value: managers and superiors of legal knowledge organizations, for instance, increasingly begin to realize that recruiting, retaining, and developing talented people is crucial to their competitive position.

One of the conclusions from my PhD study was that the organization of many major law firms is unfortunately still defined by the application of outdated, bureaucratic organizational principles which are characterized in the legal sector by a pyramid structure with a functional hierarchy and working in a joint and methodical way. Knowledge organizations, such as major law firms, are orga-

nized in such a way that they actually operate as a production factory: as soon
as you have a certain trick, you are expected to master it further and only work
on matters that concern your subject. You are placed at a conveyor belt, as it
were: you are only consulted when your advice is required. In order to achieve
scale advantages, customer contact is carefully avoided and all other possible
efficiency measures are implemented from above. And this results in unmoti-
vated employees and a high turnover of well-educated lawyers (Stand van de
Advocatuur, 2010). According to my PhD supervisor, professor Herman Kuipers,
it is structurally impossible to motivate highly educated knowledge workers in
bureaucratic organizations.

My research showed that knowledge organizations who wish to ensure that
their employees are involved and productive and wish to retain them for the
organization, must implement structural changes in their organizational design,
where questions such as autonomy, personal responsibility, freedom, and the
level of labor division must be discussed. This sounds so easy, but the daily
practice is very different. This is not surprising, as every manager has a strong
desire for control. Me included. In my own organization, we used to work with
weekly schedules that all accountants had to submit in order to meet my desire
for control. Within the legal profession, it is even common to register every six
minutes of used time per client in order to check the turnover made on
employee level.

If only I had listened to Johan Cruijff, I realized later. Although he is just as
inimitable as some of the scientific articles I read later, Cruijff made me realize
the importance of sports as a metaphor for leadership insights. Theories can be
made very insightful by means of examples from sports. Cruijff is crystal clear
about leadership: 'Create space!' And also: 'Once you know who possesses
which qualities, you must make optimal use of this. True wingers, such as Piet
Keizer, Coen Moulijn, Rob Rensenbrink, and more recently Marc Overmars;
they're still here. The point is that their return is less, because the rest of the
team, running around them, are causing trouble. The others just get in the way.'
In his book *Je gaat het pas zien als je het doorhebt* (*You won't see it till you
understand it*) he answers a question asked by Pieter Winsemius about Marc
Overmars: What is Overmars' main quality? That's right, speed. But what do
you need for speed? No, not a good start or light weight! That's useless without space. If I want Overmars to sprint in the bathroom, he won't get anywhere.

You need to have space if you want to make use of your speed.' This is not only true for sports: the same rules apply to the business world and in science; space is important. A scientist is unable to think creatively if he is limited by all sorts of methods and designs imposed on him in advance. An entrepreneur cannot do his job properly if he has to spend hours on bureaucratic rules and procedures. Space, on the other hand, is challenging.
Overmars is rock solid in one-on-one situations,' Cruijff says. 'He can pass his opponent by and is capable of giving a strong assist. But he needs space and the invitation to make use of it. It's so simple that you don't understand why people don't see it' (Winsemius, 2011).

An important addition I would like to make is that space is not limitless. Space is created by its boundaries: without boundaries, no space and no return (Tissen, 2008). Making agreements is essential to the offered space. There is a reason Cruijff always stresses the importance of discipline. 'That's why sports are so good. No rules, no game. Sports automatically include discipline. In tennis, you're allowed two serves, not three. And that white line has a purpose.' Autonomy as a prerequisite for engagement: you will only see it when you understand it.

2. Feedback
Research by Schaufeli, Taris, and Van Rhenen (2008) among managers and executives of a Dutch telecom company demonstrated that an increase of the work-related energy source 'performance feedback' was a positive predictor for an increase of engagement a year later. Feedback (and performance feedback) was defined as information that employees receive about the quantity or quality of their past performances (Prue & Fairbank, 1981). Research by Bakker (2004) also showed that managers who provided unambiguous feedback to employees brought about greater involvement and better performances.

In the business world, feedback is often formalized in and marginalized to only one or two moments per year: the evaluation and/or performance review. However, top sports consist of daily measurement and feedback: during training and matches, you can expect feedback at every moment. Not only by a coach, but also by fellow athletes. And this does not only improve your performance, but also makes you happier, according to research into engagement.
Measuring is a must. Feedback must be given as often as possible. Not only in

sports, but certainly in the business world and science as well. Without measuring there is no useful experiment, learning effect, or success experience. Feedback must be effective though, according to Jacco Eltingh. With his double partner Paul Haarhuis, Eltingh belonged to the top of tennis for years and in the heat of the match, countless indications, criticisms, emotions, and other cries were called out. Therefore, Eltingh and Haarhuis agreed on four principles about the desired form of their feedback to each other: 'Feedback must be direct, clear, vulnerable, and sincere, otherwise it doesn't work. These four principles served as our basic rules for success. If you want to get the most out of each other, the sincerity with which you share something, the directness, clarity and the vulnerability — you can do something better than I do — will bring out the best in everyone. Paul, for instance, had different talents than I did and when you discuss those characteristics and join forces in a positive way, the tone is different from when you feel you have lost and point out each other's flaws. These four principles are the essence of good feedback to me.' Eltingh's attitude and remarks form the fifth step of the step-by-step plan Become a HERO:

> **Become a HERO - Step 5**
> Deviate from the established course and take risks.
> At the same time, absorb all possible knowledge to help you along.

3. Social support
'People have to fulfil various basic needs in their work. An important one is connection, or receiving social support: people need social support from their colleagues or manager in order to be able to do their jobs well,' says professor Willem van Rhenen. From his medical background, he utilized the theory of engagement to approach psychological phenomena such as burn-out differently.

This remark by Van Rhenen reminded me of college when I met soccer player René Eijkelkamp, playing for FC Groningen at the time, and his brother Harold. During those years, I discovered more and more about both brothers and their mutual bond: René could not do without Harold and vice versa. Harold even gave up his job to drive René around to his last club Schalke 04. I was invited along once and it was an unforgettable experience. From Dalfsen to Gelsenkirchen, there was not a quiet moment. Laughter was alternated with the latest news from the region and right, René also had to play soccer. Not that he did not give it his all, on the contrary. Buckling down came naturally to him, just as

time for social relaxation. In his eyes, both facets belonged together in order to make performance possible. In the end, René even made it to the national team, where he played six international matches.

But that was not the end of his international career: thanks to his social nature and human qualities, national coach Bert van Marwijk added Eijkelkamp to the technical staff of the national team in 2011. As a striker trainer, he traveled to the European Championship 2012 in Poland and Ukraine, where he offered guys such as Huntelaar and Afellay the necessary support for their optimal performance.

Although this experience may not have been a highlight for Eijkelkamp from an athletic point of view, I must conclude that this 'ordinary' guy from Dalfsen, who was often described as rigid and was not thought to have a great future in professional soccer, had a very impressive career. After all these years, I still believe that René could never have built such a successful career without the support of his wife Loes and particularly that of his brother Harold.

To this day, Harold and René remain inseparable: they now form the duo Eijkelkamp Pro Soccer, where they guide and supervise young, talented soccer players and offer them support in their early career. When I asked René a while ago what his 'higher goal' in life was, he simply stated the following: 'Only stability: for me and the people around me. If they do well, I do well.'

4. Coaching

In the spring of 2012, I met with Toon Gerbrands at his workplace in the AZ soccer stadium in Alkmaar, to talk about the importance of good coaching. Gerbrands was active as a top-level volleyball player for years, eight of which in the first and premier league. Subsequently, he became volleyball coach and, under his guidance, various volleyball teams won no less than four national titles. Gerbrands then became the coach of the Dutch national men's team, which won a European title and also placed themselves for the Olympics in Sydney. Later, he switched to the ice skating team of DSB and nowadays he is the general director of soccer club AZ. Definitely a versatile man. With one common theme in all his activities: coaching winning teams — but also coaching uncertainty.

Gerbrands' story begins in 2009 when sponsor DSB finds itself in a crisis and goes bankrupt, due to which Gerbrands, as director of the soccer club, had to deliver a daily fight for a long time to ensure the survival of the club. Not only the circumstances were very uncertain in that time, but also the situation for the employees. A curator of a bankrupt bank with other interests than soccer, pessimists who predicted the downfall of the club, a search for new sponsors, and the media that spent a lot of negative attention on the soccer club: AZ and its employees lived between hope and fear.

In those circumstances, good coaching proved to be vital to keep the employees engaged and involved despite it all. Giving in was the last thing AZ needed. Gerbrands held many conversations with other coaches, managers, entrepreneurs, scientists and even a Benedictine monk, to improve as a coach. 'Each and every one of my heroes are winners who also had knowledge of other areas. These people are in motion during their entire life and remain vulnerable, because they never know for sure and are always looking for improvement. That is where their strength lies. Coaches who reach their success by doing the same thing for thirty years are not interesting to me. I am looking for a new type of person every day: 'the learning winner.'

> There, in the AZ stadium, I suddenly realized that I was a traveler who was walking Gerbrands' way: as entrepreneur, I was so keen to improve myself and to educate myself that I ended up in front of a class myself. To subsequently move from science to sports to learn from top-level athletes. I have always been on a journey of education, as Gerbrands stated. Now, it is time to win and overcome like Gerbrands, I told myself. And that is impossible without optimism.

We have now discussed four work-related energy sources. Both organizations and employees must be aware of the fact that these are sufficiently present. If you, as an employee, experience too few energy sources: explicitly ask your superior to do something about this. Therefore, this is step 6 in the step-by-step plan to become a HERO:

Become a HERO - Step 6
Explicitly ask your superior for more autonomy, coaching, feedback, and social support at and in your work.

5. Optimism
Esther Vergeer won the Jaap Eden Award no less than four times. This prize is awarded to the best athlete in the Netherlands, across all disciplines. She won

five gold Olympic medals and was the world champion in wheelchair tennis from 1998 until she quit in 2013. This is the reason why Esther Vergeer has become a leading example in the world of disabled sports and the Dutch face for perseverance and optimism.

Her life story, however, begins very differently: until she was six, Esther Vergeer was a girl like any other. During swimming practice, she suddenly felt very dizzy and she lost consciousness. She was taken to hospital hastily where a scan discovered that Esther had fluids of blood building in her brain which required immediate surgery. After having been hospitalized for six weeks she was allowed to go home – at that time, she could still walk.

She seemed to be returning to her life as if nothing had happened. And yet it happened again: first the dizziness, and later also complaints in her groin. During the holidays in 1989, things took a turn for the worse. She suffered from another sort of cerebral hemorrhage and needed immediate surgery again. Vergeer appeared to have a vascular malformation around her spine and her blood vessels were so weak that these could pop suddenly. This was what created the cerebral hemorrhage. To prevent the risk of fatal bleeding, Vergeer had to undergo a very risky operation. The operation was successful, but in the

'JUST SEE WHAT YOU CAN DO.
AND DON'T WORRY ABOUT
WHAT YOU CAN'T DO.'

– Esther Vergeer, wheelchair tennis player

recovery room, the doctors concluded that her legs no longer functioned and that Vergeer would be permanently disabled at the age of seven. Her parents were distraught. Esther, however, made a virtue of the necessity: in order to become familiar with her wheelchair, she engaged in sports.

The end result is well-known: she became an example to many, to the disabled in particular. She see this differently: 'Who of my age travels to the places I've been to? Who makes money with their sport? My message is simple: just see what you can do. And don't worry about what you can't do. It's all about positivity in life.'

6. Self-esteem

Leontien Zijlaard-van Moorsel is one of the best Dutch athletes of all time, perhaps even *the* best. She started her cycling career in the eighties and won an impressive four Olympic titles, nine world championships and two tour victories. After winning gold in Athens in 2004, she decided to end her cycling career. Eventually, she became Sports Woman of the Year six times and was chosen as the best Dutch female cyclist of all time.
Despite all successes, she felt like the most unhappy girl in the world. The greatest victory of her cycling career was something entirely different: beating the illness anorexia nervosa.

According to the theory of engagement, results can be stimulated by a good sense of self-esteem. A form of positive self-evaluation that indicates whether someone is capable of successfully exercising control of the environment. A good sense of self-esteem says something about resilience. Other examples of self-esteem are: optimism, stress-resistance, and self-confidence. Van Moorsel had literally and figuratively seen both extreme sides of the 'self-esteem' coin during her sports career.
When she became world champion at the young age of eighteen, she wanted more. Her main goal became to beat Jeanne Longo during the Tour de France. To achieve this, she was willing to do absolutely everything. She felt that she was not ready and in particular that she weighed too much to compete with Longo in the French Alps. Despite her successes, her self-esteem was dramatically low and, as a result, she started eating less and less. The consequence was that Van Moorsel eventually only weighed a mere 48 kilos and her body was about to give in completely. Anorexia nervosa had taken hold of Van Moorsel completely and was even about to take her life.
Only when her partner Michael Zijlaard told her he could no longer watch this self-destruction and ended their relationship, did she slowly come to her senses. With the result that she was riding her bike again a few years later. But now with an excess weight of twenty kilos! No one still believed in her chances.

'The situation for Van Moorsel is hopeless,' Jean Nelissen commented on television. Alongside the course, her father-in-law heard a spectator saying: 'What's that pig doing here?' 'Once the candle has been out, it will never burn to the full again,' director of the KNWU said in front of the cameras of the NOS, a Dutch television channel.
In this second cycling life of Van Moorsel, self-esteem proved to be her greatest strength. 'I'll have your comments for breakfast and show you just what I can do.' And that was the understatement of the year: Van Moorsel once again became world champion, won the Tour Féminin and won another gold Olympic medal. 'Never lose yourself, people, that's the message.'

7. Stress-resistance
When I think of stress-resistance as a personal energy source, I think of Bram Moszkowicz. Most people in the Netherlands have heard of him, but who really knows him? Public opinion suddenly turned against him in October 2012, when he had to cope with a series of personal attacks. The tax authorities seized his million Euro building at the Herengracht in Amsterdam, the president of the bar sued him for violation of reporting duty cash payments and even claimed his eviction from lawyer status. The attacks became increasingly personal and no method was left untouched to hammer down Moszkowicz in the press. The media had a field day and Moszkowicz seemed to be done. And just at that time, I had the 'pleasure' of meeting him at his office in Amsterdam. I was prepared for the worst. To my surprise, however, I found a relaxed and charming gentleman. 'I've faced bigger challenges,' he said jokingly. 'People can think what they want, it doesn't really bother me.' In answer to my question about how he managed to remain this calm and controlled under such pressure, he responded that his family history had taught him about relativism.
As many may know, he comes from the well-known lawyer family Moszkowicz and he is the son of the éminence grise of the Dutch criminal defense lawyer: Mr. Max Moszkowicz sr., who survived Auschwitz. 'Sometimes, I want to know how every inch of those 870 miles smelled and felt in those wagons that took my father, his sister, brother and parents from Westerbork to Auschwitz. (...) The facts are: the train left on Tuesday, September 21, 1942, eleven a.m. The locomotive pulled thirteen cattle wagons. Each wagon held approximately sixty Jews. Only my father returned' (Moszkowicz, 2012).

'I'VE FACED
TOUGHER CHALLENGES.'

– Bram Moszkowicz, LL.M, lawyer

To me, Moszkowicz, whom I also greatly admire as a lawyer, is particularly inspiring because he is always able to convey his message and mission in such a clarifying and energetic manner under extreme pressure. The future will teach us whether he was a hero in the original sense of the word – someone who excels through courage and spirit – or was foolhardy or reckless. Stress-resistance, engagement, and taking control are definitely qualities he possesses.

8. Self-effectiveness

During my classes and lectures, the aspect which summons the most questions is self-effectiveness. That was also the case for me when I first encountered the term and the model of engagement. The aspect of self-effectiveness really forms the point of departure for this book: by linking the model of engagement to sports and by using my heroes as metaphors for the various energy sources of engagement, I am able to make something abstract, like self-effectiveness, into something visual and tangible by means of sports images. Sports and heroes make it so much easier to explain certain things and they evoke powerful emotions.

Self-effectiveness was depicted perfectly in the commercial featuring swimmer Pieter van den Hoogenband, as described in a previous chapter. In my eyes, the commercial is about looking for the environment that suits you best, where you talents lie, and that what gives you energy. That is really what self-effectiveness is and that is precisely the central aspect of engagement: that is what I feel it is all about and what my definition of HERO – the highly energetic responsible operator – stands for.

After he had left the soccer field for the pool, Pieter van den Hoogenband achieved his first successes in 1993 at the Youth Olympic Days in Eindhoven. Several years later, he broke through on an international level. At eighteen, he surprised the world by coming fourth at both the one hundred and the two hundred meters freestyle at the Olympics of 1996 in Atlanta. As a swimmer, Pieter van den Hoogenband became one of the greatest athletes in Dutch history and won no less than three gold Olympic medals.

Pieter van den Hoogenband is one of my heroes in every sense of the word. What a difference your environment can make: the young Van den Hoogenband and his commercial symbolize self-effectiveness to me.

Activating your personal energy sources – self-effectiveness, optimism, self-esteem, and stress-resistance – is something you yourself are responsible for. That does not mean it is always easy, but everyone has it in them to take action and awaken the HERO in themselves. Therefore, this is step 7 of the step-by-step plan:

> **Become a HERO - Step 7**
> Activate your personal energy sources - self-effectiveness, optimism, self-esteem, and stress-resistance and take action.

Everyone possesses the energy sources discussed in this chapter to a greater or lesser extent; the energy sources that prove to be so essential for the state of engagement (Schaufeli, 2001; Van Rhenen, 2008; Bakker, 2009). My own research, for example, showed that lawyers, particularly in large organizations, experienced too little autonomy to become fully engaged. Investing in these eight sources – for yourself, but also for others – will bring you closer to happiness, as author Marja de Boer also indicates in her book *Durven doen wat je raakt (Daring to do what moves you)* (2011). She says, however: 'Engagement is not something we should define. Engagement is something you see. It looks like being in love, like a special kind of energy. And you feel it, engagement is the old-fashioned "being in good spirits". It's enjoyment and free energy.' I agree with her completely that engagement must be felt; an end goal. A personal compass – a kind of route map with stops in the shape of the abovementioned energy sources – can offer help to everyone who would like to receive more guidance along the way. The step-by-step plan included in this book can serve as such a guide. In the next chapter, I will talk about the step of how to stay a HERO.

High task demands

An important condition for remaining engaged and highly energetic is to continue to demand the very best of yourself. Personal and work-related energy sources rapidly become more important in case of higher task demands, as the theory of engagement posits. The higher the task demands, the greater your engagement. High task demands serve as an accelerator in the relationship between energy sources and engagement.

Hakanen e.a. (2005) tested this interaction between task demands and sources in a study among Finnish dentists. Their study showed that the dentists' engagement was boosted when the qualitative work pressure was high. Moreover, the appreciation from patients was especially positively related to engagement when physical strain was high. As soon as the physical strain of the dentists was high, they appeared to be capable of doing better jobs. At least, that is how their patients experienced it.
Similar results have been reported by Bakker and Bal (2009) in their study among teachers: their engagement increased when they were confronted with difficult students. These results, which can certainly also be applied to top-level sports, are incredibly relevant to the practice; the results suggest that employees

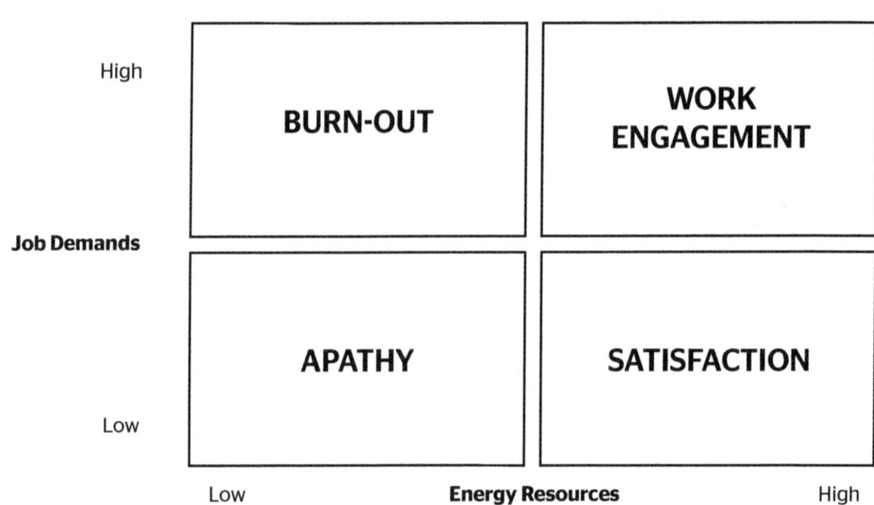

Figure 5.2: Relationships between task demands and energy sources (Bakker, 2009)

can handle a lot of work, as long as they are fed by sufficient energy sources. Research shows that task demands can even be converted into challenges and that employees become especially engaged in difficult circumstances, when the demands are high. Satisfied employees will only become engaged when there are challenges they wish to, and are able to, tackle (figure 5.2).

In order to remain a highly energetic responsible operator, you must set high standards; as high as possible. Michelangelo once said the following: 'The greatest danger is not in setting our sights too high and missing our goals as a result, but rather setting our sights too low and achieving them too easily.' The idea is to keep your final goal in mind, even if the journey seems to take forever and the end goal seems to be further away at times.

Unexpected things will happen during every journey, things that can function as a lever for new opportunities: you run into an expert in your field — at a birthday celebration for instance — who advises you to change your approach after hearing your story. Or who even wants to help you achieve your goal. The next step to become a HERO is therefore:

Become a HERO - Step 8
Turn coincidental events in an uncertain environment into levers for new opportunities. Be flexible rather than fixated on previously set interim goals. Keep only your final goal in mind.

Keeping the final goal in mind and persevering with passion and dedication applies everywhere: in sports, in the business world, and in science. I believe that no-one in my immediate circle ever suspected that I would one day get my PhD. A lot is possible, if you simply have the right attitude and make the effort, and this is often a matter of perseverance and patience.

That is certainly also true for Louis van Gaal, who did not lose sight of his end goal — playing for the world title with the Dutch team — for over ten years. In chapter 2, I already described how dramatic his first term as national coach was. But he continued to dream of a new chance, which finally arrived in 2012. He was once again hired as the national coach. At his first press conference as national coach and successor of Bert van Marwijk, he immediately made the statement: 'You have to set the bar high.' Van Gaal hoped to reach the semi-finals of the world championship of 2014 in Brazil with the Dutch national team: a very challenging objective given the disappointing results at the European

championship in Poland/Ukraine. 'Soccer son' Stijn Schaars described Van Gaal as follows:
'He is incredibly critical, demands the full hundred percent, always. Also of himself. He is never satisfied with 'sufficient', he wants perfection. I have never seen him give a training for the sake of the training. He wants full effort and commitment, and is always talking about imagining. You must visualize the higher goal' (Van Gaal, 2009).
His right hand at Bayern München, Andries Jonker, about Louis van Gaal: 'The demands are high every single day, and players feel that immediately. New players always have to get used to this, they're not used to such high demands.'
Van Gaal pushes his players to the limit, but if they succeed it makes them feel great, they know what they have all done it for. Even players who did not make it will seldom make a critical remark: they are all surprised that their levels have substantially improved and they have managed to reach this higher level thanks to Van Gaal.

Setting a high bar gives you energy and will eventually lead to life happiness. Who does not want to be part of a winning team or organization? High task demands lead to challenging work and satisfaction. And because the work or the goal is so challenging, employees develop a sense of pride and they identify themselves with achieving the higher goal. Perfectly befitting with the ancient quote by Michelangelo.

6
Act

You will only reach the top with courage and dedication, according to Ronald Naar. Courageous behavior appears to be a requirement for engagement. Arnold Bakker, professor of Labor and Organizational psychology at Erasmus University, said the following on this topic: 'In order to experience true happiness and satisfaction, you must do something, perform something, look for your boundaries. You will then use your qualities and you will find extra motivators to perform a job well. And if that is successful, you will experience a sense of happiness that goes beyond the brief satisfaction you feel in an amusement park or when watching TV or a movie. That is also a form of relaxation, but much more fleeting' (in: Hart en Ziel, 2007). This chapter is therefore about the importance of heroic behavior for an engaged life. Despite all the fears that often seem to accompany heroic behavior, such behavior is less risky than doing nothing. And this offers support in overcoming these fears.

Fight or flight, but never freeze

We know three main motivators for behavior: fight, flight, and freeze (Cannon, 1929). This was already applicable thousands of years ago on the Savannah: fight, flight, but never freeze. A dangerous animal or person would immediately punish such an attitude.

The same principles still apply today. Both within top-level sports and entrepreneurship, stagnation is decline and the competition will certainly beat you at some point. Although not everyone will want to be an entrepreneur or top-level athlete, the rules of the savannah still apply to us all, and that includes those who are looking for more happiness and satisfaction. To live with engagement, you will have to take action. That seems easy, but behavioral change is very difficult. It often occurs that we are seized by a fear to change things or to persevere with something difficult, after which we put the desired goal on hold. The stress hormone cortisol is the reason why we subconsciously exchange the necessary attitude — fight or flight — for freeze. Improved vitality, and especially an increase in the 'sports hormone' endorphin, make it easier to take mental action as well. By taking physical action, preferably with endurance sports, you produce endorphins which help you to overcome your fears and take on new challenges and opportunities. Only by remaining fit can you overcome your fears and get closer to your end goal.

Engaged individuals are able to overcome their fears and that is the next step towards achieving their end goal. And that is why step 9 of the step-by-step plan is as follows:

Become a HERO - Step 9
Overcome your fears and keep to your course.
Use uncertainty as a condition for actions to be taken.

All heroes I have interviewed all told me the same thing: there were so many days and moments that it was almost too much for them and when they wondered why on earth they were doing it. However, they felt there was no alternative for their calling, for instance to become a world champion.

Various studies indicate that 60 to 80 percent of all absence through illness have nothing to do with illness, but rather with demotivation, a lack of enjoyment and internal involvement. The societal expense caused by problems at work are estimated to come close to 5 billion Euros per year (Instituut voor Werk en Stress, 2012). I have never regretted my decision to become an entrepreneur and quit my job. The opposite, in fact: I do not think I would have been this engaged and energetic these past fifteen years if I had not taken that decision.

I believe that if fear is preventing you from fully developing your talents, you will eventually become washed out. Courage is a must. There is no other option. Think of the Epke Zonderland's exercise at the high bar at the Olympics of 2012: 'Epke is not the gymnast of ultimate grace and perfection. His style is based on a big heart: speed, strength, agility and gumption,' says sports coach Marc Lammers. 'As an entrepreneur, success can only be achieved by letting go of the high bar every now and then.' Epke Zonderland showed an exercise with three consecutive flight elements in the finals, something that had never been done before. His courage was rewarded with a gold medal and he became the greatest Dutch hero of the Olympics that year. And yes, I realize that that is easier said than done.

'IN ORDER TO FEEL REAL HAPPINESS AND SATISFACTION, YOU MUST ACT, PERFORM SOMETHING, LOOK FOR YOUR BOUNDARIES. YOU WILL THEN USE YOUR QUALITIES AND FIND EXTRA MOTIVATORS TO PERFORM A JOB WELL.'

— Prof. dr. Arnold Bakker, Erasmus University

Courage is a must. This is also the idea I had when I started my own enterprise at the age of 27. I knew it wouldn't be easy, but entrepreneurship and creativity were my passion, I simply had to go for it. The thought of all possibilities and creativity this demanded gave me boundless energy. It felt as a calling I couldn't run from; no matter how many arguments I could come up with. But it was sometimes certainly trying.

At moments like those, I thought of how I must feel to have to go to a twelve-story office building every day and perform the plans from some board I didn't know. I immediately realized: entrepreneurship is my calling, I must persist! And when I take a look at my own high bar, following Epke Zonderland, I see that I have only managed to achieve success by letting go and raising the bar. No matter how scary that was, it was essential for moving forward.

What is courageous behavior?

I have spoken of courageous behavior, but how can courageous behavior or courage be defined? Courage is really nothing more than beating your fears, one might say. True heroes are not characterized by the absence of fear, but rather by the will to overcome this fear, as Canadian psychologist Stanley Rachman also states. He studied the distinction between being fearless and courageous. Ranchman followed 105 parachutists in training. Only a quarter of them experienced no fear before their first jump, but the rest had indicated they were slightly to extremely tense beforehand. And yet, they all jumped. Afterwards, the quarter of parachutists who had not been afraid were still not afraid, but the nervous group could be subdivided into two groups; a large group who had overcome their fears due to this experience and felt confident about their next jump, and a small group of 7.5 percent, who had been terrified and never wanted to do it again. The majority of the parachutists had jumped despite their fear, and facing their fear had made them less afraid. For Rachman, these were the true heroes and he gave them the label 'brave' (Rachman, 1989; *Psychologie Magazine*, 2012).

Courageous behavior can also be displayed unexpectedly, as social psychologist Zimbardo discovered. Under his supervision, 24 volunteers, all people who had been evaluated as perfectly normal, were gathered for a prison experiment in 1971: the first twelve were appointed as 'guards' of the other twelve, the 'prisoners'. Zimbardo had designed the experiment to be able to study for two weeks what would happen in such a social situation and to observe who would display which type of behavior under such difficult circumstances. After a mere six days, the experiment was terminated because things were getting out of hand; the guards were behaving like animals. Zimbardo, however, was not the one to stop the experiment; it was stopped by a brave young student who resisted the experiment and refused to conform to the hierarchy that exists at college. Despite the fact that this student had everything to lose, she bravely went against her superior and thwarted his experiment. Zimbardo concluded that, not only are we all capable of doing bad things when the situation brings out the worst in us, but we are apparently also capable of courageous behavior.

'TRUE HEROES ARE HESITANT HEROES. PEOPLE WHO DO KNOW FEAR, BUT CAN FIND THE WILL TO OVERCOME IT.'

– Prof. dr. Stanley Rachman

In his book *The Lucifer Effect* (2010), Zimbardo discusses various ways of thinking we can use to tap into our heroism. His most important clue is to create more distance between yourself and the situation: we often hardly perceive 'wrong' situations, which arise gradually, as such and they do not seem to affect us. According to Zimbardo, heroes distinguish themselves by 'perceiving' actively at the moment of action: they are convinced that the things they see affect them and that looking away is not an option, because it makes you morally culpable. That such a situation may make you terrified is less relevant: after all, no one expects you to be fearless. Quite the opposite.

Courageous behavior requires energy and nonconformity

Research conducted by Angela Crott also indicates that courageous behavior has to do with energy, and not just with courage. In 2012, she obtained her PhD for her thesis *Van hoop des vaderlands naar ADHD'er (From the hope of the fatherland to ADHD)*. Crott studied books on the upbringing of boys that had been published between 1882 and 2005. Her conclusion: rascals have always existed, but what we called 'wantonness' in the past is now labelled anti-social behavior. 'Where boys used to be valued for their gumption and physical energy, they are nowadays stuffed with Ritalin. (...) And that is a shame, because it was precisely this type of person which acted in case of societal or personal need.' Crott describes an example from the moment that she, in her previous career as a teacher, had become stuck on gymnastics apparatus during gym class. It was the most disobedient boy in class who was brave enough to rescue her from her uncomfortable position; the other children watched in silence. The brat became the hero.

'WHERE BOYS USED TO BE VALUED FOR THEIR GUMPTION AND PHYSICAL ENERGY, THEY ARE NOWADAYS STUFFED WITH RITALIN.'

– Dr. Angela Crott

Heroes are not just people of the highest moral standing. Because what would you call someone like Jabbar Gibson, for instance? On September 1, 2005, this twenty-year-old American stole a school bus to save the lives of many people in completely flooded New Orleans. He was the first to deposit the victims of hurricane Katrina safely outside the affected area; due to failing help, the last people were helped five days later. A true hero, but surely also a rascal: on September 1, 2005, this young man singlehandedly

confiscated a school bus, and drove this bus from New Orleans to Houston without a proper driver's license. And that while he already had a record for car theft, possession of drugs, and an armed robbery…
And yet, Jabbar perfectly suits the image of heroes that has arisen these last years from psychological research. That these are recent findings is not at all surprising; heroism and courage were mainly the field of historians and philosophers in the past. Psychologists were more interested in fear. The emergence of positive psychology changed this. Nowadays, psychologists are equally interested in why people do brave things. Even if it is only to learn why people who act despite their fear seem to develop anxiety disorders less often (from: *Psychologie Magazine, 2012*). Those studies have already provided a few notable insights. For instance, that the capacity to act quickly and decisively in dangerous situations is indeed greater for Jabbar-like people. Not that good citizens always fail in such situations, but the initiative usually lies with energetic, more self-willed types of people.

There is a reason why true heroes are rare. Most of us conform to our environment and think twice before they rush headlong into a dangerous situation. That was not the case of Marco Kroon, the only official hero in this book. From March to August 2006, Kroon was sent to the Afghan province of Uruzgan as platoon commander. His task was to explore the area, so that the Task Force Uruzgan could be built. During a nine-day patrol, Kroon encountered a group of Taliban fighters. In the gun battle that followed, he requested air support. He had his men take cover and personally guided the American fighter planes to the enemy, which were less than ten meters away from him. The Americans created a dangerous situation: large and small pieces of metal flew past him, but miraculously, he remained unharmed. Later that night, he managed to repel various Taliban attacks from an Afghan house.

During all of the fights which he participated in, no one at his side died and he managed to ensure that his colleagues respected the dead and the wounded. These actions and also his general performance as supervisor moved his colleagues and superiors to recommend him for the Military Order of William. After an investigation lasting two-and-a-half years, the Order was awarded to Kroon on February 10, 2009, and on May 29, 2009, he was knighted in the Military Order of William Fourth Class.

ABOUT MARCO KROON:
'HE DOES NOT RECEIVE THIS AWARD FOR A SINGLE ACTION, BUT FOR HIS WORK AS A LEADER, A COMMANDER, AND A HUMAN BEING.'
— Queen Beatrix

By speaking the oath: 'I shall conduct myself as a faithful and valiant knight' and the knighting by Queen Beatrix, the Netherlands had a new Knight in the Military Order of William for the first time in over fifty years. Queen Beatrix stated the following reasons upon bestowing the award: 'He does not receive this award for a single action, but for his work as a leader, a commander, and a human being during the entire mission.'

In the spring of 2012, I spoke to Marco Kroon about the subjects of courage and dedication. His statement that courage and dedication seemed to come naturally to him during professional actions, but that private troubles stretched him to the limit was surprising to me.

After his full-time position with the Ministry of Defense, Kroon managed a bar in Den Bosch with his then girlfriend. On January 30, 2010, it became known that the Public Prosecutor had issued an investigation on the suspicion of a violation of the Opium Act and the Weapons and Ammunition Act. Kroon publically fell from his pedestal and had to fight a different fight entirely: about his own innocence. During the first hearing, it became clear that possible traces of cocaine were found on Kroon's chest hair, his coat and in his pockets.
A settlement for the possession and passing on of electroshock weapons, where the Public Prosecutor would waive further prosecution if Kroon admitted to the possession and use of cocaine was rejected by Kroon. It would have saved him a lot of heartache if he had given in, but he did not conform. On the

contrary, he announced that he would hand in his Military Order of William if he were to be found guilty. We now know the results: Kroon was acquitted for possession of drugs and had to pay a fine for the possession of an electroshock weapon in his bar.

'To me and those around me it was really very simple,' Kroon said. 'In a personal conversation with general Van Uhm, I have admitted to having this electroshock weapon in my bar right from the start. It made me feel safe. I have never had anything to do with drugs though.' Later: 'What made it hard was the public opinion: suddenly, I was the villain, rather than a decorated war hero.' The queen did not share this opinion. She continued to support Kroon: 'After general Van Uhm had informed the queen of my predicament and my statements, she sent me a weekly message of encouragement. What a wonderful woman.'

Kroon's story is a typical example of current findings regarding courageous behavior. Professor in clinical psychology Peter Muris, for example, discovered that children who scored high on his courage test (the Courage Measure for Children), scored lower on the personality dimension agreeableness; potential heroes are less inclined towards obliging behavior. How very applicable to Marco Kroon: if he had simply given in, he would not have had to deal with the entire case and accompanying publicity. Heroes are not afraid to go against public opinion and to face the accompanying risks.

Effectuation as a theory to achieve your goal

The Austrian-British philosopher Ludwig Wittgenstein (1889-1951) constructed the formula W/A = B, where W stands for will, A stands for *angst* or fear, and B for *bereich* or reach. A simple formula any top-level athlete and entrepreneur will understand. To achieve something, you must overcome your fears and that is only possible if your will is strong enough. Or, as Ten Bos (1997) phrased it: 'You mustn't only dare to rely on a good feeling or on intuition, you must also dare to convey this intuition.' The theory of effectuation was very helpful to me in overcoming my own fears. The Indian Saras Sarasvathy stands at the cradle of the effectuation theory. For her PhD at Carnegie Mellon University in Pittsburgh, she studied how successful entrepreneurs worked. She discovered five recurring principles of success that are perpendicular to what we have always been taught. These are the principles of effectuation. Sarasvathy describes effectuation as 'a type of human problem solving that considers the future as fundamentally unpredictable, but controllable through human action: the environment as constructible by choices and goals as negotiable outcomes of stakeholder commitment rather than an pre-existing ordering in preferences' (Sarasvathy, 2001).

Already in kindergarten we are taught the importance of logical order and causal explanations. However, as the crisis has shown us, it is very questionable whether the future can be described and explained so logically. Entrepreneurs who are effective and successful in uncertain environments do not subscribe to the illusion of predictability. Effectuation offers insight into a more effective and flexible attitude. The five principles of Sarasvathy's research are detailed below.

'THERE ARE **FIVE PRINCIPLES OF SUCCESS** THAT ARE PERPENDICULAR TO WHAT WE HAVE ALWAYS BEEN TAUGHT.'

– Dr. Saras Sarasvathy

---

1. Bird in Hand Principle

Think from the available means and not from goals. Do not wait for the perfect opportunity. Take action, based on what is immediately available. You take stock of the available means by virtue of the three W-questions: know who you are (know your proposition), know what you know (and also what you don't know), and know who you know (enter into partnerships). This very important message from the effectuation theory forms step 10 in my step-by-step plan of becoming a HERO.

2. Affordable Loss Principle

What is it worth to you to advance an idea? Also think of whether the investment is acceptable, in other words: do not invest more than you can risk. Do not
take too big a risk, where you only consider possible high future profit.

3. Lemonade Principle

Make coincidental events in an uncertain environment into levers for new
opportunities: 'If you come across lemons, make lemonade!' Stay flexible rather
than being fixated on existing goals.

4. Crazy Quilt Principle

Forge strategic alliances and partnerships (collaborative relationships) with people
and organizations (stakeholders) who each contribute to the eventual, unpredictable quilt in their own way. Select the right partners who are prepared to enter
into a real commitment by letting them invest what they can afford. Do not worry
too much about the competition, nor about complicated strategic planning.

5. Pilot in the Plane Principle

Focus on what you can control and create your future with that. If you make
your own future (effectuation), there is no need to predict or control it.

Effectuation offers managers and professionals concrete handles to structurally
use and stimulate brave behavior. Thomas Blekman, teacher at Rotterdam
School of Management, is viewed as the advocate of effectuation in the Netherlands. He considers effectuation to be a young approach to boost internal entrepreneurship and innovation within large enterprises, a way to prevent that innovation only comes from laboratories that are often completely closed off from
the outside world. 'Nowadays, market research and spreadsheets all too often
form the guideline for strategic decisions,' says Blekman, who wrote the book
Corporate Effectuation. 'A credit crisis, tax alterations, or a ban on smoking may
trip everything up in that case. Effectuation is a way of arming yourself against
such unpredictable events.' (MT, 2011)

By applying the five principles of effectuation companies are much better able to remain in control of new projects if unexpected situations arise. It is not about predicting the future, so that the future can be controlled, but by partly shaping the future, so control becomes unnecessary. Countless studies, however, teach students the principles and means of causality (causal reasoning). Unfortunately, this view seems to be opposite to the vision upon which successful entrepreneurship is based. The starting point of causal reasoning begins with a specific goal and one looks for the means to achieve this goal. In practice, successful entrepreneurs, such as Hennie van der Most, reverse this idea; they hold onto their final goal and trust their intuition that sufficient opportunities will arise.

Sarasvathy also refers to effectuation as 'the logic of the experienced enterpriser'. Perseverance and an eye for new opportunities appear to be inextricably linked to business success. Neuropsychologist Erik Matser posits that people who are capable of allowing their intuition to direct their knowledge and experience, are exceptionally suitable to excel. A property that is also of crucial importance in top-level sports. Lionel Messi is not physically the strongest soccer player, but he is exceptionally able to see where the space is and to anticipate on this. He has the unique talent to 'read' the situation and the match. Individualists such as John McEnroe or boxer Mohammed Ali also proved to be masters in intuition. This goes to show that this has nothing to do with intelligence or analytical capacity, but rather with intuitive insight and the inner peace to recognize this insight. Just like Hennie van der Most or Richard Branson, who did not have any education at all. At the age of sixteen, the dyslexic British businessman had had enough of school. His performances in class were substandard, but as an entrepreneur Branson was highly suitable.

Every success is relative, however: today's winners are tomorrow's losers. And vice versa. It is not about how often you fall, but how often you get back up again. Michael Jordan, the tallest basketball player in American history, says on this subject: 'I have missed over 9000 shots on the basket in my career. I have lost over 300 matches. 26 times I was given the faith to win the match with my penalty, but I missed. And that is exactly why I booked so much success.' My definition of HERO is therefore not about the success or failure experienced today, but about the attitude that brings personal success and a joyful life.

7

Self-knowledge

The importance of work-related and personal energy sources and high task demands for engagement have been discussed in the previous chapters. In order to become and remain a HERO, self-knowledge is essential, as various studies indicate (including, Buckingham, 2006; Bakker, 2007; Pink, 2010; Kodden, 2011).

Naturally, it is interesting to know which energy sources you must have at your disposal to become engaged. After all, engagement leads to better performance and more happiness in life. But that does not mean that you can simply flip the switch with that knowledge: now I will become an optimist! Or: now I will become stress-resistant. Self-insight and self-knowledge are necessary to know what can make you more optimistic or stress-resistant. We all possess unique energy sources that can help us do so, we only need to be able to place them and tap into them.

'The personal energy source as dependent variable of your personal motivators', as scientists have attempted to formulate such a simple causal relationship in a rather difficult way. The one (your motivators) leads to the other (tapping into more energy sources). By looking at ideals, motivators, meaningfulness, way of responding, qualities, pitfalls, and prohibiting patterns with mildness and acceptance, you make contact with the basic energy that belongs to you specifi-cally.

Self-knowledge: get to know your own unique energy sources with the enneagram

In order to discover what your motivators are — your basic energy as I call this — various theories and tests are available, but I would like to introduce you to the enneagram. The enneagram provides you with a manual for understanding yourself and others better. It is an instrument that allows you to find your own unique basic energy. And you can use this basic energy to do the things that suit you, that give you energy, and can make you into a HERO with more opti-mism, more stress-resilience, and more self-esteem. From the day we are born, we all respond to our environment differently and we all have different goals. Sometimes, we hardly understand why we do what we do and why we are not like others. Let alone that others understand us. Or we them.

The main thing the enneagram has given me, in addition to a user manual, was a 'clear mirror'; the enneagram is harsh in the plusses and minuses that belong to each personality type. But it also teaches you to handle your own unique basic energy in a conscious and 'healthy' manner and to avoid your pitfalls.

Introduction to the enneagram

The enneagram is an age-old instrument that was given new life by the famous Stanford University near San Francisco. Stanford is one of the top universities in the world and both their research and education are held in high regard. Various Stanford graduates have played an important role in the development of Silicon Valley and made this place into the world's most important center for the high-tech industry. William Hewlett and David Packard, for example, were two Stanford researchers who started up one of the most renowned electronics and computer science companies in history, right from the garage of their home in 1939: Hewlett Packard.

The instrument is really nothing more than a model that describes nine personality structures. We call these the enneagram types. These can be thought of as nine different glasses through which people look at the same reality. The basic concept of the enneagram is that each type has a subconscious motivator. Something that is very important deep down. It automatically determines where one's attention goes. In doing so, it determines one's pattern of thoughts, feelings, and actions. This is the reason why you will respond in a similar manner to certain events. Everyone has such a fixed pattern with automatic tendencies, the contents of this pattern are however different for each of the nine types Although you can certainly have personality traits that belong to other types, there is always one dominant type. Whether this type is genetically determined is uncertain, but many believe that this type has already been formed before birth. The enneagram theory was not only created regarding the search for different types and the relationships with others, but also for a healthy development within your own type.

The nine types (or 'enneagram types', *ennea* means 'nine') are universally denoted with the numbers 1 to 9. These types are shown here:

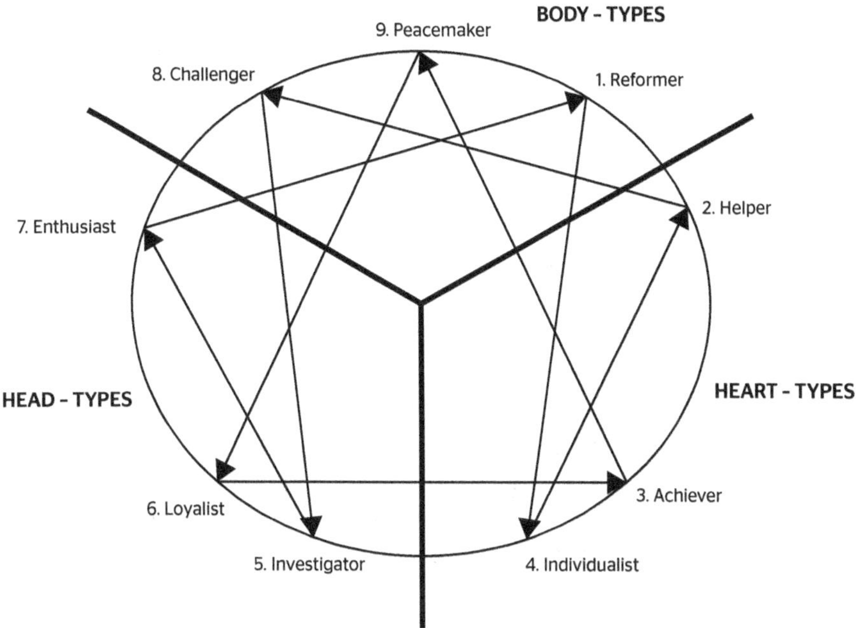

Figure 7.1: The enneagram

The personality types can first be subdivided into three main groups:
1. the body – types
2. the heart – types
3. the head – types

The three groups and nine individual personality types will be discussed below, where I will make use of information from various websites (including www. enneagram.nl, www.enneagramcollege.nl, www.eclecticenergies.com, and www. scar.dds.nl).

Few people are truly balanced. Finding that balance is the most difficult task we are facing in life. The enneagram theory describes the following three operating centers: body, heart, and head. Also referred to as: anger, sadness, and intellect. Every person has a part of these three centers. The level of development of these three centers is often unbalanced. For everyone there is one center that is most developed, another that is a little less developed, and a third that is hardly existent. People who are very physical — the body types — know anger and respond from their body; their gut. They often do not think before they act and they do not follow their hearts. They completely fail to understand those that respond from the heart. Those people know sadness and feel with their chest. They react completely differently than those in the third group, who work from the head. They think and respond from fear or from challenging fear.

Body types (the motor center)

Were you very physical, quick, and active as a child? Than you are in the motor center, at the 8, the 9, and the 1. In this motor center, or body center, when a situation arises people first experience bodily sensations before they are capable of thinking or feeling. The basic energy or motivator of these body types is to take a position against something. This manifests itself in aggressiveness at the 8, in stubbornness at the 9, and in critical perfectionism at the 1.
The people in the motor center are characterized by anger. Those who recognize themselves in the body center often have problems with their head (anger).
If you are a body-oriented type, you generally filter the world through your intelligence, your sensations, and your instinct. You use your personal position and power to create life as you feel it should be. You invent strategies that ensure your place in the world and that reduce inconvenience as much as possible.

If you belong to the motor center or if you feel attracted to it, you run the risk of your feelings not being fully heeded, because you always become restless. You do feel, but before you can do something with it, other things seem to happen. Perhaps you want to take action too quickly. You can also fail to take action, but rather feel a sort of apathy when you have connected with your feelings.

If you feel well and there are no problems, it is easy for you to use your feelings. But sometimes the feelings become blocked and a force arises that demands immediate results. This can also be accompanied by an emotion that is akin to anger; or nothing at all happens and you seem to be lost in daydreams. Because you are a physical type, you wish to convert your feelings into actions immediately. But given the fact that these feelings arise best in a state of peace, the best exercise is focused on peace.

Heart types (the emotional center)

The basic energy of these three types (2, 3, and 4) goes out to others to be able to gauge feelings. The number 2 is looking for love, the number 3 for admiration, and number 4 wants to be understood. Perhaps you remember that you were very emotional as a child. If that is the case, you probably belong to the emotional center and chances are that you have enneagram type 2, 3, or 4. People within the emotional center display their feelings through sadness. The three types within the emotional center are characterized by confusion, a type of identity crisis. If you are a heart-oriented type, you generally see the world through the filter of emotional intelligence. You are attuned to the feelings and emotional state of others in order to maintain the sense of connectedness to them. More so than the other types, you are dependent upon the approval and recognition of others for your sense of self-esteem and to support the feeling of being loved. In order to ensure approval and recognition for yourself, you create an image of yourself that encourages others to accept you and feel you are special.

Naturally, not only heart-oriented types are dependent upon emotional intelligence to develop the higher qualities of the heart center, such as empathy, understanding, compassion, and loving kindness, but these three types are characterized by this, which is less so the case for other types.

If you belong to the emotional center, there is a good chance that your emotions will not be balanced with your head: you are sometimes overcome by emotions. You sometimes lose your feelings and become tied up in the expression of it, the emotions. What you must learn is how to regulate these emotions. You have to give them a place where they no longer negatively affect your feelings, but support these instead.

Head types (the intellectual center)

Each of the three personalities (5, 6, and 7) within the head type experiences the world as an overwhelming, frightful, or calculating place. Their basic energy appears to be oriented inward: the 5 isolates himself in his thinking, the 6 withdraws, and the 7 refrains from commitment and pursues activities in his constant search for new stimuli.

If you used to be very good at school as a child and used your head a lot, there is a good chance your enneagram type can be found in the intellectual center.

The types from the intellectual center are characterized by suspicion, because they operate on the basis of fear. Those who find themselves inside their heads often have stomach issues at a young age (fear).

If you are a head-oriented type, you generally view the world by means of your mental capacities. This strategy aims to minimize fear, control potentially painful situations, and create a sense of security by means of thought processes such as analyzing, anticipating, imagining, and planning. Naturally, not only head-oriented types are dependent upon mental intelligence for the development of the higher qualities of the head center, such as wisdom, knowledge, intuition, and depth, but the head-oriented types are characterized by these. If you belong to the intellectual center, you could have problems reaching your emotions, because it is difficult for you to trust them: after all, it is your head that does all the work. You can trust your head. Yet, you often have good ideas, where you look for an intellectual explanation for a feeling. You attempt to reason emotion, which makes it more difficult for you to realize that it concerns an emotion. You automatically translate this to your brain. Therefore, it is very important to become aware of your emotions.

Enneagram type 1 - The reformer
Reformers, or perfectionists, feel responsible and are fixated on improvement.

People with this personality type are essentially looking for a way to improve things, because they never feel anything is good enough. This makes them perfectionists who wish to reform and improve; idealists striving to create order in the ever present chaos.

Number Ones have a great eye for detail. They are always aware of the flaws within themselves, in others, and in the situations they find themselves in. This activates their need for improvement — which may be beneficial to all those involved, but which may be equally burdensome for both the Number One and those who are at the receiving end of One's attempts to reform.

Number One's incapacity to reach the perfection he desires feeds his feelings of guilt and failure and his emerging anger about the imperfectness of the world. However, Ones have the tendency to feel guilty about their anger. Anger is a 'bad' emotion and Ones genially strive with their whole hearts to be 'good'. Anger is therefore forcefully supplanted, interrupted by incidental bursts of anger, but it usually manifests itself in one of the many less noticeable varieties such as impatience, frustration, annoyance, and judgmental criticism. For this reason, Ones are sometimes rather difficult to live with, but they also tend to be loyal, responsible, and capable partners and friends.

Regardless of their profession, they are active, practical people who get things done. They are born organizers: people who make lists and actually finish every single thing on the list. The last one to leave the office, the first one to be back in the morning. Diligent, reliable, sincere, and dutiful.

Their continual pursuance of the ideal means that Ones sometimes find it difficult to relax and unnecessarily deny themselves many harmless pleasures of life. They tend to be emotionally inhibited and feel ill at ease in expressing tender feelings: in general, they view emotion as a sign of weakness and a lack of self-control. They are rarely spontaneous. They do however have various interests and talents: they are independent and seldom have nothing to do.

Ones are often intelligent and independent. They can easily be mistaken for Fives, but unlike Fives, Ones are first and foremost people of action, not of thought. Ones have a tendency to worry, are sensitive to fear, and can sometimes be wrongly labeled as Sixes, but they do not have the same inclination to join a group and their norms do not arise through seeking consensus in a group.

Finally, the continuous pursuit of perfection can take its toll and lead to a depression. A typical example of this is Leontien Zijlaard-van Moorsel: in her struggle for perfection, she took it so far that it brought her close to self-destruction. 'Eventually, I weighed a mere 48 kilos and I still felt too heavy to beat Jeanne Longo in the Tour de France.' Her fight for perfection brought out both the worst and the best in her.

Have you ever wondered why Louis van Gaal and Johan Cruijff argue as they do? They are both personalities of type One: the reformers. Ones are serious people and are generally exceptionally principled, competent, and without compromise. Because they believe in their convictions with such passion, they are often excellent leaders who inspire those who follow them with their own vision of excellence. Or not! Recognizable?

Famous Ones: Johan Cruijff, Louis van Gaal, Leontien Zijlaard-van Moorsel, Nelson Mandela, Dalai Lama, and Hillary Clinton (source: www.enneagram.nl).

Enneagram type 2 – The helper
Helpers who need to be needed

People of this personality type essentially feel that they are valuable insofar as they are helpful to others. Being altruistic is their duty. Being able to give to others is their reason of existence. Involved, socially conscious, usually extravert – Twos are the types of people who never forget a single birthday and who will always do their utmost to help a colleague, spouse, or friend in need. Twos are therefore warm, emotional people for whom personal relationships are essential, who put great energy into these relationships and who expect to be appreciated. They are practical people who thrive in care-oriented professions. Helping others makes Twos feel good about themselves. Being needed makes them feel important; altruism makes them feel virtuous. A large part of the self-image of Twos is regarding these matters and a threat to that self-image is hardly tolerated. Twos are deeply convinced of their own altruism and it is true that they are often truly helpful and caring towards others.

Twos need to feel needed: their love is therefore not entirely without ulterior motives. Because they have stuck out their necks for others, Twos feel that they have a right to gratitude. They can become pushy and demanding if their emotional needs, which are go unrecognized, are not satisfied.
They can be bossy and manipulative and even feel that this is justified as they 'have earned this right' and their intentions are good. The darkest side of this fixation emerges when Twos start to feel they will never receive the love they deserve for their efforts. In such circumstances, they can become hysterical, irrational, and even insulting.

Because Twos generally help others to satisfy their needs, they might forget to attend to their own needs. This can lead to physical burn-out, emotional exhaustion, and emotional caprice. Twos must learn that they can really only be of use to others if they themselves are healthy and balanced.

Twos could label themselves incorrectly if they are not actually in a clear helping role, particularly when they cannot see their level of involvement. In such a case, male Twos are often thought to be Ones or Threes, the neighbors of type Two (the adjacent types are referred to as 'wings' in enneagram theory). Women of all types have a tendency to recognize themselves in the dynamics of type 2 in their personality, because such qualities are socially rewarded. Female Nines, for instance, run the risk of being incorrectly labeled Twos, especially when they are the mothers of young children. Where Nines have a tendency to be self-effacing and humble, Twos are proud and have a strong sense of self-worth.

The most famous Twos? Mother Teresa and Bishop Desmond Tutu (source: www.enneagram.nl).

Enneagram type 3 - The achiever
Focused on the achievement of success, to be valued

People within this personality type seek confirmation to feel valuable; they pursue success and want to be admired. They are often hard workers, with a competitive nature and are very focused on pursuing their goals. Whether their goal is to become the most successful salesman in the company or to be the 'sexiest' woman in their social circle. They have often worked their way up and usually find some area in which they can excel in order to find the external approval they so desperately need.
Threes are socially competent, often extravert, and sometimes charismatic. They know how to present themselves, are confident, and have a practical and driven attitude. Threes have ample energy and often seem to embody a type of zest for life that is very appealing to others. They are good networkers, who know how to rise in rank. But although Threes tend to have success in every field they focus their energy on, they are often secretly afraid of being or becoming losers.

Threes sometimes have trouble finding intimacy. Their need to be confirmed in their image hides a deep feeling of shame about who they truly are, shame which they subconsciously fear will be revealed when others come too close. Threes are often generous and captivating, but it is difficult to truly know them. When they are emotionally unhealthy, their narcissism may become ugly and they could become coldblooded and ruthless in the pursuit of their goals.

Because external confirmation is central in the type Three-fixation, Threes often try — either consciously or subconsciously — to embody the image of success that is promoted by their culture. Threes get into trouble when they confuse actual happiness with the image of happiness promoted by society. When a Three has a 'good' job and 'attractive' partner, he could— through self-deception and self-betrayal — be prepared to ignore his inner impulses that tell him that neither his job nor his partner fulfil his deeper needs. Even the most 'successful' of Threes, who generally seem to be fairly happy, often hide a deep sense of meaninglessness. Achieving an image of success is never really satisfactory.

Threes can sometimes incorrectly label themselves when they view the more shallow traits of their personality as indicators of their type. An intellectual Three, for instance, could incorrectly label himself as a Five; a female Three, dedicated to her role as a mother, could think that she is a Two. A Three in a leadership's position could incorrectly be labeled as an Eight, and so on. However, regardless of the manifestation, the core of the type Three-fixation is the deep need for external confirmation and achieving the established goals.

The most famous Three I know? Erben Wennemars! Looking at this more closely: apparently, I have always admired Threes for a reason, and Erben in particular. I recognize myself most in the type Three with all its advantages and disadvantages.

Enneagram type 4 - The individualist
Identity seekers, sensitive, individualists

People of this personality type tend to build their identity around the perception of themselves and the idea that they are unique or different in one way or another: they are very self-conscious and individualistic. Fours have the tendency to consider their distinction as both a gift and a curse: a gift because it distances them from those they view as 'ordinary' in some way, and a curse because it so often seems to remove them from the simpler forms of happiness that others appear to enjoy so easily. Fours manage to feel superior to others, while at the same time harboring some level of yearning and envy. The feeling of being a member of the 'real aristocracy' is alternated with deep feelings of shame and fears of somehow being flawed or imperfect.

Fours are emotionally complex and very sensitive. They yearn to be understood and valued because of their authentic self, but easily feel misunderstood and unvalued. They have a natural tendency to withdraw, in the face of the world that seems harsh or rough, and are often moody and fickle. They seem to be immersed in their own emotions and spend a large portion of their lives submerged in their own sensitivities, which they feel free to cultivate and analyze. A desire to realize this internal world often leads to an interest in art and various Fours actually become artists.

Whether they are artistic or not, most Fours have a feeling for esthetics and are interested in self-expression and self-revelation. Whether this concerns the clothes they wear or the general nature of their, often wayward, lifestyles.

Fours are somewhat melancholical in nature and under stress they have a tendency to fall victim to depression. Furthermore, they have the tendency to be introverted, even under the best of circumstances. When they become unbalanced, they are prone to self-leniency, which they consider to be fully jusitified and to compensate for the general lack of fun they experience in their lives. Instead of looking for practical solutions for their problems, Fours often tend to fantasize about a savior who will rescue them from their unhappy existence.

Intellectual Fours often tend to incorrectly label themselves as Fives. Fours, however, have a tendency for self-revelation and are at ease with emotional expression, something Fives certainly are not.

Famous Fours? Herman Brood, Princess Diana, and Michael Jackson (source: www.enneagram.nl).

Enneagram type 5 - The investigator
Thinkers, tend to withdraw and observe

People of this personality type are afraid that they do not have enough inner strength to face life. Consequently, they tend to withdraw and go back to the safety and security of their own minds, where they can mentally prepare for everything that is coming.

Fives feel comfortable and at home in the world of their thoughts. In general, they are intelligent, well-read, and deliberate and they often become experts in

the fields of their interests. Although they are sometimes scientifically oriented, particularly if they have a Six wing, it is not at all uncommon for Fives to have artistic tendencies. Fives are often slightly eccentric: they feel little need to change their convictions to adapt to the opinion of the majority and they refuse to have their freedom of thought restricted.
The problem for a lot of Fives is that, while they are at ease in the world of thought, they are usually far less comfortable in the world of emotions, the requirements of a relationship, or the need to find a place for themselves in the world. Fives tend to be shy: they do not want to impose, wish to be independent, and are often unwilling to ask for other people's help, while they would probably be glad to offer help themselves.

Fives are sensitive: they sometimes feel ill equipped to face the world. To compensate for their sensitivity, Fives sometimes adopt an attitude of careless indifference or of intellectual arrogance, which unfortunately results in the creation of distance between them and others. Attempting to bridge that distance can be difficult for Fives, because they seldom feel comfortable with social skills. If they do succeed, they are often dedicated friends and lifelong companions.

Few people knew what is going on beneath the surface of Fives, because they have an almost exaggerated need for privacy, plus a deep-rooted fear of intrusiveness. Due to their sensitivity and fear of inadequacy, Fives fear to be overwhelmed by the demands of others or the force of their own emotions. By developing a minimalistic lifestyle, in which they require little of others — in exchange for little being required of them — they try to compensate this. Other Fives make peace with the unpleasant messiness of life and are more involved, but they nearly always retain their fear of the thought that life will somehow ask more of them than they can give.

The most famous Fives? Isaac Newton, Charles Darwin, Friedrich Nietzsche (source: www.enneagram.nl).

Enneagram type 6 – The loyalist
In conflict between trust and mistrust

People of this personality type feel unsafe, as if nothing is stable enough to hold onto. At the core of the type Six personality lives a sort of fear or dread. This fear has a deep source and can manifest itself in various ways, which does not make Sixes easy to describe and classify. However, all Sixes share the fact that fear is deeply rooted in the center of their personality, which manifests itself in worrying and restless predictions of everything that could go wrong. This tendency gives Sixes a talent for troubleshooting, but it also robs them of the peace of mind they so desperately need. It can also make their personality lose spontaneity. The essential fear at the core of the type Six-fixation appears to suffuse the personality with a sort of 'defensive suspicion'.
Sixes do not trust easily: they are often ambivalent about others until the moment that person has absolutely proven himself, at which moment they will most likely respond with a steadfast loyalty. The loyalty of the Six, however, has something of a double-edged sword, because Sixes tend to support a friend, partner, or job long after it is time to move on.
Sixes are generally looking for something or someone to believe in. Combined with their general suspicion, this gives rise to a complicated relationship with authority. The side of the Six that is looking for something to believe in is often very receptive to the seduction to transfer authority to an external source, whether this is in the form of an individual or in the form of a religious belief. However, the Sixes' tendency for mistrust and suspicion thwarts every form of belief or authority. There are two opposite forces at work in the personality of enneagram type Six and those forces may take on different shapes.

When labeling Sixes, it is confusing that there are two fundamentally different strategies Sixes use in order to cope with fear. Some Sixes are primarily phobic: these Sixes are generally accommodating, easily join in on something, and have a cooperative nature. Other Sixes use the opposite strategy to cope with fear and become 'counter-phobic': a provocative attitude toward anything they see as threatening. Counter-phobic Sixes can be aggressive and adopt a rebellious or anti-authority attitude, rather than look up to authority. Counter-phobic Sixes are often unaware of the fear that motivates their own actions. In fact, Sixes generally tend to be blind to the extent of their own fear.

Because Sixes are unaware of the extent of their own fear, they often label themselves incorrectly. For example, female Sixes may label themselves as Twos, in particular when they identify themselves with a role as helper. Sixes, however, have a much more ambivalent attitude about relationships than Twos, who generally know exactly what they want.
Sixes who do not recognize their fear may incorrectly label themselves as Nines, but Nines have the capacity to relax and trust others, which is a difficult task for Sixes. Sixes may also classify themselves as Fours, especially when they have artistic tendencies, but do not become immersed within themselves as Fours do. They can also incorrectly classify themselves as Fives, in particular when they are intellectual —as many Sixes are — but contrary to Fives, Sixes often have a practical nature. Finally, counter-phobic Sixes may easily and incorrectly label themselves as Eights, but they lack the self-confidence of Eights.

The most famous Sixes? George Bush, David Letterman, and Richard Nixon (source: www.enneagram.nl).

Enneagram type 7 - The enthusiast
Pleasure seekers and planners, looking for distraction

People of this personality type would like their lives to be one big exciting adventure. Sevens are restless people, oriented at the future, who are generally convinced that they can find something better right around the corner. They are quick thinkers, who have a great deal of energy and who make a lot of plans. They tend to be extravert, are often multi-talented and creative, and have an open mind. They are enthusiastic, enjoy sensual pleasures and do not believe in denying themselves anything.

Sevens are practical people with a wide range of skills. They know how to net-work and how they should promote themselves and their interests. They often have an enterprising attitude and are capable of transferring their enthusiasm to those around them. When they are able to focus on their talents, they often become very successful.
However, focusing is not always easy for Sevens. Their tendency to believe that something better is still waiting for them, makes them hesitant to limit their options or to pursue their goals with true dedication.

The central problem for Sevens is that they pursue pleasure in a compulsive way. Sevens are fear types who are particularly afraid of the power of negative mental states. They avoid these states by seeking distraction in their external environment: by doing multiple things simultaneously, by keeping their options open, by looking for all sorts of stimulation. For this reason, Sevens are more sensitive than most to addiction: whether this is to shopping, gambling, drugs, or anything else.

Sevens have a tendency to think highly of themselves and their talents: they tend to focus on their strong suits and downplay their faults and flaws. They are often a little selfish, which manifests itself in a strong sense of justification. Because Sevens are unwilling to face their own dark emotions, it is also difficult for them to experience and acknowledge the pain of others, making it hard for them to see the reality of other people. The extent to which Sevens flee from negative emotions is a measure of the mental health of Sevens: the more a Seven runs from this, the stronger the negative emotions grow and the more likely it is that they eventually burst in the form of an anxiety disorder or serious depression.

Because they look outward and are not given to introspection, it is not unusual for Sevens to classify themselves incorrectly. Sometimes, they incorrectly label themselves as Eights, because Sevens can be dominant. But Eights are not fearful as Sevens are. Sevens may also easily believe they are Threes, but Threes are more determined and do not desire to keep all their options open. Surprisingly, Sevens may also incorrectly classify themselves as Fours: when they see the difference between the optimistic, pleasure-oriented person they project to the rest of the world and their own, often fearful, internal mental states, they can confuse their pain with the melancholy of type Four. Sevens flee from this pain, however, whereas Fours often cultivate their negative mental states.

The most famous Sevens? John F. Kennedy, Tom Hanks, Eddie Murphy (source: www.enneagram.nl).

Enneagram type 8 – The challenger
Eights take charge because they do not want to be controlled

People of this personality type do not want to be controlled: not by others and not by their own circumstances. They seek to fully be in control of their own destiny. Eights are strong-willed, decisive, practical, firm, and energetic. They also tend to be dominant: the wish not to carry out the will of others often manifests itself in a need to control others instead. However, when they are mentally healthy, they are able to keep this tendency in check. The tendency is always there, however, and may take on a central role in the interpersonal relationships of the Eight.

Eights generally have powerful instincts and strong physical desires, which they surrender themselves towards without guilt or shame. They want to take what they can from life and are fully prepared to do what it takes to bring that about. They need to be financially independent and have difficulty working for someone else. Most Eights make peace with society, but always retain a sense of discomfort in any hierarchical relationship in which the Eight is in another position than the top.
It is difficult for Eights to give up their defense in intimate relationships. Intimacy brings emotional vulnerability and this vulnerability forms one of the deepest fears of the type Eight. Betrayal, in any kind, is absolutely intolerable to them and this can bring about a powerful response from the wronged Eight. In the field of intimate relationships, Eights' control problems are clearly apparent, in which matters of trust play a crucial role.

Eights have a sentimental side they often do not show to those around them, for fear of becoming vulnerable. But although trust is difficult for an Eight, when an Eight truly lets someone in, he becomes a steadfast ally and loyal friend. The powerful protective instincts of the Eight come to the surface when it is necessary to defend friends or family and Eights are often dangerously generous in supporting those they care about.

Eights have a tendency towards anger. When they are seriously provoked, or when their personality is not well balanced, bursts of anger can change into rage. Emotionally unhealthy Eights can be aggressive and can even be violent when under pressure. These Eights enjoy intimidating others who they perceive as 'weak' and feel little remorse in bulldozing over those who get in their way. They can be harsh, cruel, and even dangerous.

It is more likely for female Eights to classify themselves incorrectly than it is for male Eights, as many of the typical characteristics of the type Eight personality are often discouraged in women in our society. Other types usually confuse themselves with Eights. This is particularly the case for male counter-phobic Sixes, who do not realize that their aggression is a cover for underlying fears. Sevens also tend to incorrectly label themselves as Eights, but Sevens lack the intensity of the strong focus that characterizes the type Eight. Although both Sevens and Eights have a lot of energy, Eights have a physically-based energy, while the energy pattern of a Seven has a nervous, mental quality.

Famous Eights? Franklin Roosevelt, Norman Schwarzkopf, and Joop van den Ende (source: www.enneagram.nl).

Enneagram type 9 - The peacemaker
Keeps the peace and harmony

People within this personality type have a need for peace and harmony. They tend to avoid conflicts at any price, whether this concerns an internal or inter-personal conflict. Because conflicts naturally occur in life, Nines have the tendency to withdraw in order to prevent conflict.
Many Nines are introverts. Other Nines lead a more active social life, but always remain withdrawn to a certain degree in order to protect themselves from external threats. Most Nines are relatively easygoing: they adopt a strategy of 'going with the flow'. In general, they are reliable, firm, self-effacing, tolerant and sympathic people.
Nines tend to adopt an optimistic approach to life: they are generally trusting and see the best in others. They often have a deep-rooted trust in the idea that things will turn out well. They desire to be connected, both to other people and to the outside world. They often feel most at home in nature and are generally warm and thoughtful parents.

The Nines' incapacity to tolerate conflict is translated into a conservative approach to change. Change can evoke unpleasant feelings and disrupt the

Nines' desire for comfort. Less healthy Nines are often incapable of motivating themselves to take action and to bring about an effective change. However, when change comes, which will generally happen, Nines notice that they are perfectly able to adjust: they are often more resilient than they think.

In fact, Nines generally have low self-esteem. This self-effacing attitude appears to be an invitation for others to take them for granted and to fail to recognize their (important) contributions. This can result in a subsurface anger that builds up in the psyche of the Nines, leading to incidental tantrums that soon pass. Being overlooked is a source of deep sadness for the Nines, a sadness they hardly know how to express.

Nines often classify themselves incorrectly, because they have a somewhat diffuse sense of their own identity. This is reinforced by the fact that Nines often merge with the people they love and because they take on characteristics of the people close to them. Female Nines often incorrectly label themselves as Twos, in particular when they are the mothers of young children. Nines tend to be self-effacing, though, while Twos are relatively aware of their own self-worth. Nines also often confuse themselves with Fours, but Nines tend to avoid negative emotions, while Fours often intensify those. Intellectual Nines – men in particular – often incorrectly classify themselves as Fives, but Fives are intellectually non-conforming, while Nines are focused on reconciliation and wish to avoid conflict.

Famous Nines ? Helmut Kohl, Walt Disney, and Ronald Reagan
(source: www.enneagram.nl).

Special thanks to Willem Jan van de Wetering of Enneagram College for providing his type descriptions. Van de Wetering is an authority in the field of personal development and the author of over thirty books in this field.

Using your basic energy

Would you like to know what personality type you have? At Stanford, the SEDIG test (Stanford Enneagram Discovery and Inventory Guide) was developed by Dr. David Daniel: in fact the only reliable and scientifically supported test which helps you to discover your unique basic energy. The test is available on: www.eclecticenergies.com/nederlands/enneagram/test.php. The enneagram is not only a descriptive model, but certainly also a tool for development: every type in the enneagram corresponds to higher qualities — often also referred to as virtues — that provide a guideline for development. In conclusion of this subject, I can very much recommend that you further acquaint yourself with this instrument to increase your self-knowledge and basic energy. *The book Werken met het Enneagram — naar persoonlijk meesterschap en sociale intelligentie* (Working with the Enneagram — towards personal mastery and social intelligence) by Hanna Nathans (2000) is a book I like to use myself and can highly recommend.

Everyone possesses a certain amount of basic energy, which you can employ for different matters. In this chapter, I showed how and why you could use that energy to get to know your personal motivators and talents: it provides you with a lever of personal — and connected work-related — energy sources. This positive flow of energy, that is optimally utilized for personal motivators and talents, makes you engaged, highly energetic, and happy, as the theory of engagement states (Bakker, 2009). Every day, you will experience the will to pursue your personal goals: you can become a true HERO. If you set the bar high enough for yourself!

The give and take of leadership

Although this book is more about taking the lead than it is about leading — which, in my eyes, is only natural as taking the lead is so much more important and difficult and leadership is based on authenticity — I would be remiss if I left the new leadership role undiscussed. The most important tasks for leaders are recruiting and selecting engaged top talents — the future heroes — and especially managing the already present energy and making as many work-related energy sources as possible available.

I believe that developing energy and talents is the most important goal of a leader; not managing, but developing new talents. Not controlling present energy and talents, but tapping into new energy and talents: it is precisely this mind-shift which leads to success, happiness, and wellbeing. The current C-leadership style — commanding, communicating, and controlling — must be exchanged for a D- leadership style: the development of goals, the development of talents, and the discharge of energy. The CEO as Chief Energy Officer.

Recruiting and selecting engaged top talents

Although top talent has always existed, the interest for recruiting *the best and the brightest* fluctuates greatly. During a recession, the focus lies on reducing expenses. This is understandable, but also unwise, according to Ralph Knegtmans, managing partner at De Vroedt Thierry (2011). In these times, short life cycles of products and services require a new approach. The greatest effects by means of cost savings have already been realized. You can now only differentiate by having the right top talents. Useful recruitment of talent comes down to an optimal match between the person, the organization and the energy this creates. But how do you recognize tomorrow's heroes? After all, there is no universal talent for all situations, everything is context dependent.

As discussed in previous chapters, criteria can be formulated by means of which you can recognize the highly energetic responsible operator and which leaders can use for selection. Here are ten of such criteria:

1. Passionate

Unfortunately, the cognitive side is still over-appreciated. Particularly IQ, competencies and branch experience are still disproportionally considered. As previously discussed, intrinsic motivation and passion have proved to be more valuable as indicators of future success. The HERO radiates this passion.

2. Brave

A HERO deviates from the established courses and takes risks. He realizes that not taking risks is in fact a greater risk to him and his organization.

3. High absorption capacity

A HERO eagerly absorbs all knowledge made available to him. The HERO can be completely absorbed in his work, in a pleasant way.

4. Authentic

A HERO is an independent thinker with his own work style, who makes use of his own unique and authentic talents. He usually adds something extra to the customary business models.

5. Taking the lead

Thanks to personal energy sources such as self-worth and stress-resistance, the HERO has a proactive attitude, he does not wait until he gets an assignment, and he fulfils his duties with independent thoughts to achieve the final goal. He has often already developed his own masterplan.

'DO IT! NOW!
GET IT DONE! EXCUSES
ARE FOR WIMPS.'

– Tom Peters, 'guru of the management gurus'

---

6. Vital and dedicated

A HERO can be recognized by his vitality and dedication: he is full of energy, feels strong and fit, and is able to work long and tirelessly. He is also very involved in his work and radiates pride and enthusiasm about the work he does.

7. Self-starting

A HERO is able to activate his personal energy sources and start a plan that is not yet fully developed and detailed.

8. Development-oriented

A HERO is oriented on development and explicitly requests more coaching and feedback from his supervisor in order to make larger developmental steps.

9. Flexible

A HERO is flexible and makes coincidental events into a lever for new opportunities.

10. Action-oriented

A HERO does not wait for the perfect moment, but takes action with the means he has at his disposal.

Top talents cannot excel at everything. The one may excel in his trade, while the other is perhaps more of a generalist who manages to connect the various fields. They can often do things people are already good at even better. Making top talents into heroes: that is what should drive every leader.

Managing talents

Through the years, I have gained ideas from many management gurus. I have absorbed them all, but in particular those of Tom Peters. His book *In Search of Excellence* had been in existence for 30 years in 2012. Although the book was first published in 1982, all the basic principles are still fully applicable today. Peters' view provides a sense of grip in these uncertain times. He states that leadership is not about control, but rather about creating a joint journey of discovery: the grand finale, as I like to call it.

'AFTER EVERY
PERFORMANCE, YOU
MUST FIRST DISTURB
THINGS,** THEN RECOVER
IN ORDER TO GROW.'

– Erben Wennemars

It is all right to make mistakes. In fact, making mistakes is essential, according to Tom Peters. When you do not make mistakes, he says, you simply have not reached far enough. A nice way to look at it, which perfectly suits Michelangelo's quote about setting the bar too low.
Another reason for my admiration of Peters work concerns his vision on leadership: good leaders create more and better leaders. This is something I greatly believe in. But leadership nowadays has become a lot more complicated compared to thirty years ago, as professor Daan van Knippenberg from Erasmus University indicates: 'Previously, leaders worked according to the "command & control" model. This model has become outdated because work and the organization of work has changed.' Present-day leadership is more about empowerment, both of the leader himself and of his team. It is about letting go of the old, familiar ways of thinking and embracing new thoughts and actions. Space for making independent decisions and carrying responsibility. 'A good leader will make sure there is unison and that the whole team carries the same mission,' according to Van Knippenberg. When asked, he states that a lot of organizations still have a control reflex. 'This is a natural management reflex, but it's less functional — particularly in the case of matters that are not controllable.'
A balance between freedom and control is indispensable for a good leader. And yet, the essence of good leadership remains: bringing out the best in your people to realize the best results. However that must now be brought about in a faster changing and less predictable world. Therefore, you should give your people space.
Thirty years ago, the 'boss' really was the 'boss'. Nowadays, a leader has a more facilitating role; thinking of ways to tap into his people's energy and managing to employ this energy for organizational purposes.

The CEO as Chief Energy Officer

Management is top sport which means that managers must adopt the attitude of corporate athletes, states Jan van Zwieten, director of the Mentally Fit Institute. Managing energy rather than time leads to fit, durably employable and more effective managers and employees who manage to keep burn-out at bay. Leaders would better be called Chief Energy Officers, rather than Chief Executive Officers.

> Research among senior managers:
> - 47% is overweight
> - 20% does not do any form of exercise
> - 32% often feels lonely
> - 25% believes that his health seriously affects the organization
> - have a 3.4 times greater chance to develop a burn-out than someone with lower work pressure
> - more than 90% of these senior managers do not talk about these themes for fear of a negative effect on their career
>
> National Institute of Health, CBS 2010

Van Zwietens basic motto is 'Manage energy, not time'. As far as I am concerned, this should become the basic rule for every modern leader; I support it completely. It is not about booking as many hours as possible, but about improving your productivity. 'Less is more', as various studies show. A Finnish study into dentists, also a traditionally burn-out sensitive profession, demonstrated that as soon as dentists started to exercise for two and a half hours a week, instead of working these hours, their productivity increased (Van Thiele Schwarz e.a., 2011). In the Netherlands, the managers of Ernst & Young were confronted with this productivity paradox: while partners worked more and more hours, the number of declarable hours decreased. Furthermore, over 30% appeared to show signs of a burn-out. To turn the tide, they implemented an experiment in which partners were not allowed to work for more than four hours a day. Despite the fact that their worktime had been cut by half, they seemed to perform just as much as they did during a normal workday. It seems that managers must learn to effectively utilize both their own time and that of their employees. And not increase the pressure by making everyone keep running around, without wondering whether their energy is being well used.

Managing vitality and energy

According to Van Zwieten, managers, like top athletes, can learn to attune their agenda and eating pattern to the physiological calendar, their natural daily rhythm. This calendar has two energy peaks that are alternated with less energetic periods, such as the circadian depression: the natural low after lunch, which is less low after a healthy meal. 'A lot of managers, however, have a cheese sandwich and a glass of milk for lunch and plan a difficult job or important meeting at half past one,' Van Zwieten says. Whereas they will book less results at that time than they will during the energy peak from 14.30 to 16.30. The energy during that peak is often lost, however, because they are distracted by employees dropping in or phone calls and emails. Therefore, it is important to learn to make sure that you are not disturbed during those two hours of energy.

The body needs sufficient time to recover from the daily efforts. After all, there is a reason top-level athletes go to bed early. Human beings need at least six hours and preferably eight hours of sleep. On average, the Dutch sleep seven and a half hours per night, but many leaders and employees fall short of this number.
'Many managers overtax themselves. Especially the X and Y generations want it all: a successful career, a beautiful house, two cars in the driveway, going on holiday three times a year, a nice family and a busy social life.' This requires enormous physical and mental efforts that tear down their energy, according to Van Zwieten. 30 to 40 percent of the Dutch population have sleeping problems, and nearly 1.5 million people use sleeping pills. The Dutch suffer from burn-out at an increasingly younger age. 'Those who sleep well every night and exercise three times a week will not experience burn-out,' Van Zwieten states.

Sleeping well is not just about the quantity of sleep, but mainly about quality. It is best to go to bed around 22.30, because the body will start to create the sleep hormone melatonin at this time which halts the brain for a deep sleep. While we are sleeping, the production of growth hormones and creatine and the uptake of vitamins and minerals ensure that our physical battery is recharged. About 80 percent of time spent sleeping goes into recharging the physical battery, subdivided into four blocks of time. If you go to bed at midnight, you will catch the second 'train' of melatonin and miss out on the most important and largest block of physical recovery. Therefore, the advice is to stop earlier and get up earlier in the morning to finish something, rather than finishing it late at night. Being busy before going to bed may also hinder our ability to fall asleep and therefore makes recovery more difficult. Light, for instance from a laptop screen, inhibits the production of melatonin. For this reason, Van Zwieten advocates putting your laptop away at 10 PM and make sure that you use the half an hour of 'care time' before bed to clear your head of all thoughts. Only then can we bring about full physical recovery and is there time left for the mental-emotional recovery that occurs later on during our sleep, in the lucid phase between dreaming and waking. This phase reorganizes memory, anchors learning processes, and reduces stress. The dream sleep can also be invoked during the day. 'Think of powernaps, or yoga and meditation. By closing off your consciousness to all external stimuli, you create brief moments of recovery.' Those who cannot recover due to a lack of sleep and relaxation will experience fear, irritation, and stress during their workday more often (from: *Management Executive*, 2011).

According to Cannon (1929), there are three main motivators for behavior in case of danger: fight, flight, or freeze, motivators that we have inherited from the Neanderthals. All responses are controlled by the production of hormones. Adrenaline gives us the energy and courage to fight. Cortisol and growth hormone, on the other hand, are stress hormones that make you freeze. By exercising, you can manage your own positive energy. By moving intensively, the body releases adrenaline and endorphins which give you a happy feeling. If your life is standing still, both literally and figuratively, you constantly press the cortisol pump which will make you feel very stressed. There is a reason all burnouts are cortisol driven. Stress levels can also be measured by means of your heart rate and hormone levels.

Whether it concerns leaders or employees: energy can be managed. By managing energy on the one hand, and controlling stress on the other hand, people are capable of realizing the same results with less effort. In addition to the traditional role of planning and control, modern leaders are expected to adopt the role of coach and mentor and to keep track of the energy levels of their teams. The CEO as Chief Energy Officer.

In 2010, I let go of my enterprise after twelve and a half years of building, failing, persevering, and building again and passed it on. Not only because I felt the organization could do with some fresh energy, but also because I felt I did not have the right energy to do this again myself after so many years. I also wanted to focus on conducting scientific research and educating young, ambitious professionals to become future leaders: the new heroes in my view. Letting go of my enterprise felt like a huge risk: what was I giving up? The question that immediately surfaced, however, was: but what will I get in return? In my case, it was the room to pursue my passions and find a better use for my talents. The decision was clear: let's do it! 'You must not be afraid to renew,' said Esther Vergeer. 'That is something that is true for both athletes and entrepreneurs. And that in combination with daring to take risks. The risks are part of it!'

'DARING TO RENEW IS SOMETHING THAT MATCHES BOTH AN ATHLETE AND AN ENTREPRENEUR. THIS IS OFTEN ACCOMPANIED BY TAKING RISKS.'

— Esther Vergeer

The power of energy management

The labor market is rapidly changing and in the next thirty years, the potential professional population will decrease by three quarters of a million, according to the CBS (the Central Bureau of Statistics). While the number of elderly people increases, the number of working people decreases. This requires sustainable and wide employment of the total present amount of available energy, also at a macro-economic level. Consequently, employers and employees must take their responsibility and make sure that they utilize this energy optimally. I believe in the power of energy management as contributing towards sustainable employability and wide talent development. Vitality of body and mind, and care and attention to these factors are essential components of self-development and development of your talents. A strategic view on energy management, that is carried on both the highest and the lowest level in the organization, is a prerequuisite. Sustainable talent development plays an essential role here. Employees are motivated, stimulated, and facilitated to work on their own fitness and vitality.

Involvement from all departments, the board, and possibly also the board of directors and support from a work's council are a determining factor for success. Everyone must contribute to energy management. A fitness program, set up specially and attuned individually, must not be seen as an expenditure, but as an investment that will redeem itself in various fields. A program at Ernst & Young resulted in employees becoming 85 percent fitter, 75 percent had improved their stamina, and 63 percent of participants experienced a better energy balance. 51 percent indicated that they were able to work in a more focused way as a result.

Vital people perform better and enjoy things more. According to research conducted by Diehl and Stoffelsen (2007), vital employees do not only look happier, they also seem to do things with little or no effort, have practically no complaints, recover faster, and have plenty of energy left at the end of the day.

Vitality and energy management sound much more positive to most people than the words health and working conditions. Who does not want to have more energy left at the end of the day? For instance to exercise.

Step-by-
step plan
for the
HERO

Discover the HERO inside yourself. Learn your own talents, personal goals and your unique personality type and become a true HERO: Someone with total passion, energy and punctuality in life and who is able to pursue his personal goals. In this book I have provided a ten-step plan to achieve your goals. For reference, I will list them here.

Step 1
Discover and deploy your authentic talents. Your zest for life and energy will increase significantly.

Step 2
Draw up a masterplan and develop a final goal for those topics that tap into your talents and passions.

Step 3
Make sure that you enjoy the things you do and remain fully dedicated to your final goal.

Step 4
Make sure you are both physically and mentally fit, so that you can create additional energy. Stick to your master plan, but always remain open to new ideas.

Step 5
Deviate from the established course and take risks. At the same time, absorb all possible knowledge to help you along.

Step 6
Explicitly ask your superior for more autonomy, coaching, feedback, and social support at and in your work.

Step 7
Activate your personal energy sources - such as optimism, self-esteem, stress-resistance and effectiveness - and take action.

Step 8

Turn coincidental events in an uncertain environment into levers for new opportunities. Be flexible rather than fixated on previously set interim goals. Keep only your final goal in mind

Step 9

Overcome your fears and keep to your course.
Use uncertainty as a condition for actions to be taken.

Step 10

Think on the basis of the available means and not on the basis of goals.
Do not wait for the perfect opportunity. Take action, based on what is immediately available.

More information and free articles on leadership and enthusiasm can be found on www.sebastiaankodden.com or www.baskodden.nl

After-
word

Kurt Lewin's saying that nothing is as practical as a well-formed theory has always inspired me to continue my studies as an entrepreneur. Eventually, I even ended up with a new career path. As experienced entrepreneur and young doctor, I eventually found the time to publish a book about my fifteen years of practical experience and my proven theory of enthusiasm.

The book is written for anyone who is interested in ways to improve one's enthusiasm in life. Naturally, in practice this isn't always that easy, as affirmed by famous athletes, coaches and entrepreneurs. The book provides concrete and proven tools to assume a positive attitude in life, allowing you - full of energy and passion - to start working on new plans as soon as tomorrow. The fact that less than twelve percent of the Dutch labor force experience this feeling of enthusiasm in their work was a huge stimulus for me to start writing this book, instead of leaving theory to theory and practice to practice.

While writing, one question always stuck with me: after all those years, had I become a enterprising scientist or a scientific entrepreneur? Unfortunately, I couldn't find any suitable role models who I could connect with and use as a mirror. In the end, this was something I had to discover for myself. Looking back, the writing of this book proved to be a wonderful form of positive self-therapy. After months of writing and exploration, I came to the realization that I didn't necessarily have to make a decision between the two but could simply remain myself: enthusiasm is created when you are able to combine your energy sources with your personal talents and motivations, while simultaneously finding the right environment. It was precisely the combination of science and entrepreneurship that gave me pleasure and energy and also formed the environment in which I could be effective. During my journey, I discovered my very own 'blue ocean', just as Kim & Mauborgne (2005) have described: an area where few other fishermen have gone; where you can distinguish yourself and add new value. Not the choice, but the combination eventually proved to be the key to my own enthusiasm: the opportunity to teach young entrepreneurs and managers and being able to transfer knowledge and experience.

As Joop van den Ende dictated earlier: you must sharpen your focus, if not, you will lose yourself. Looking back, I firmly believe his remark to have been the most valuable to me. Surrendering my first company several years ago felt like a huge risk. However, at the same time it also gave me new energy and the opportunity to grow my educational talents to a new wisdom.

132

Thanks to this book - and remembering the words of Confucius — my inspiring trip ended in a fabulous homecoming. A big thank you to all my travelling companions for this beautiful experience.

References

References

• Akker, P. van den (2012). Sporten maakt je slim. Geraadpleegd op http://www.bnr.nl/radio/199617-1205/sporten-maakt-je-slim.
• Bakker, A.B., Demerouti, E. & Verbeke, W. (2004). Using the Job Demands-Resources Model to Predict Burnout and Performance.
Human Resource Management, 43(1), 83-104.
• Bakker, A.B. & Bal, M.P. (2010). Weekly Work Engagement and Performance. A Study Among Starting Teachers. Journal of Occupational and Organizational Psychology, 83, 189-206.
• Bakker, A.B. & Demerouti, E. (2009). The Crossover of Work Engagement Between Working Couples. Journal of Managerial Psychology, 24, 220-236.
• Bakker, A.B. (2009). Bevlogenheid in organisaties. Een model om bevlogenheid te bevorderen. Tijdschrift voor Opleiding & Ontwikkeling, 11, 15-19.
• Bakker, S. (2010). Een cursus slim werken waar je energie van krijgt. Geraadpleegd op http://www.intermediair.nl/carriere/doorgroeien/competenties/een-cursus-slim-werken-waar-je-energie-van-krijgt.
• Boer, M. de (2011). Durven doen wat je raakt. Zaltbommel: Uitgeverij Thema.
• Bos, R. ten (1997). Strategisch denken. Zaltbommel: Uitgeverij Thema.
• Breukelen, H. van (2011). Winnen. Van talent naar topspeler. Amsterdam: Atlas Contact.
• Buckingham, M. & Clifton, D.O. (2006). Ontdek je sterke punten. Utrecht: Spectrum.
• Cannon, W.B. (1929). Bodily Changes in Pain, Hunger, Fear, and Rage. New York: D. Appleton & Co.
• Collins, J. (2001). Good to Great. Why Some Companies Make the Leap... And Others Don't. New York: Harper Business.
• Collins, J. (2011). Great by Choice. New York: Harper Business.

• Covey, S. (2010). De zeven eigenschappen van effectief leiderschap. Amsterdam: Business Contact.
• Crott, A. (2011). Van hoop des vaderlands naar ADHD'er. Het beeld van de jongen in opvoedingsliteratuur (1882-2005). Proefschrift RU Nijmegen. Geraadpleegd op http://dare.ubn.kun.nl/bitstream/ 2066/91316/1/91316.pdf.
• Csikszentmihalyi, M. (1975). Beyond Boredom and Anxiety. San Francisco, CA: Jossey-Bass Publishers.
• Csikszentmihalyi, M. & LeFevre, J. (1989). Optimal Experience in Work and Leisure. Journal of Personality and Social Psychology, 56(5), 815-22.
• Csikszentmihalyi, M. (2007). Flow. Psychologie van de optimale ervaring. Amsterdam: Boom.
• Dewulf, L. & Vangronsveld, G. (2012). Help! Mijn batterijen lopen leeg. Een burn-out krijg je niet alleen, kies voor je talent. Tielt: Lannoo Campus.
• Ericsson, K.A. (1996). The Road to Excellence. The Acquisition of Expert Performance in the Arts and Sciences, Sports and Games. Mahwah, NJ: Erlbaum.
• Evans, D. (2012). Risk Intelligence. How to Live With Uncertainty. Florence, MA: Free Press.
• Fullagar, C.J. & Kelloway, E.K. (2010). Flow at Work. An Experience Sampling Approach. Journal of Occupational and Organizational Psychology, 81, 595-615.
• Gaal, L. van, Heukels, R. & Jonker, A. (2009). Louis van Gaal, Biografie & Visie. Publish Unlimited.
• Gerbrands, T. (2011). Inspiratie, coachen & presteren. Beilen: Pharos Uitgevers.
• Gladwell, M. (2008). Outliers. The Story of Success. New York: Little, Brown.
• Hakanen, J.J., Bakker, A.B. & Demerouti, E. (2005). How Dentists Cope With Their Job Demands and Stay Engaged. The Moderating Role of Job Resources. European Journal of Oral Sciences, 113, 479-487

• Haney, C., Banks, W.C. & Zimbardo, P.G. (1973). A Study of Prisoners and Guards in a Simulated Prison. Naval Research Review, 30, 4-17.

• Judge, T.A., Vianen, A.E.M. van & Pater, I. de (2004). Emotional Stability, Core Self-Evaluations, and Job Outcomes. A Review of the Evidence and an Agenda for Future Research. Human Performance, 17, 325-346.

• Karasek, R.A. (1979). Job Demands, Job Decision Latitude, and Mental Strain. Implications For Job Redesign. In: Administrative Science Quarterly, 24, 285-308.

• Karasek, R.A. & Theorell, T. (1990). Healthy Work. New York, NY: Basic Books.

• Kim, W.C. & Mauborgne, R. (2005). Blue Ocean Strategy. How to Create Uncontested Market Space and Make the Competition Irrelevant. Boston, MT: Harvard Business School Press.

• Knegtmans, R. (2011). Diversiteit als uitdaging. Amsterdam: Boom.

• Knegtmans, R. (2008). Toptalent. Amsterdam: Boom.

• Kodden, S.F.G.P. (2011). Dedication. A Study to Analyse the Effects of Organizational Design on Employee Engagement and Knowledge Productivity Within Dutch Legal Service Firms. Breukelen. Nyenrode Press. http://www.nyenrode.nl/FacultyResearch/research/ Documents/Dissertations/kodden-bas-dissertation-abstract.pdf.

• Kroon, M. (2012). Leiderschap onder vuur. Utrecht: UHB Uitgevers.

• Kuipers, H., Amelsvoort, P. van & Kramer, E. (2010). Het nieuwe organiseren. Alternatieven voor de bureaucratie. Leuven: Acco.

• Lewin, K. (1951). Field Theory in Social Science. Selected Theoretical Papers. D. Cartwright (ed.). New York: Harper & Row.

References

- Mackenbach, J. (2010). Ziekte in Nederland. Gezondheid tussen politiek en biologie. Amsterdam: Reed Business.
- Maister, D. (2001). Practice What You Preach. Florence, MA: Free Press.
- Meijer, L. (2007). Leven zonder werk geen hemel. Psycholoog Arnold Bakker keert zich tegen fabeltje van lekker luieren: 'Als je werkelijk iets presteert, voel je voldoening.' de Volkskrant, Hart en ziel. Geraadpleegd op http://www.hartenziel.nl/artikel/leven_zonder_werk_geen_hemel/print.
- Naar, R. & Lippmann, T. (2007). Naar de top. Den Haag: Adventure Communication.
- Nathans, H. (2000). Werken met het Enneagram – naar persoonlijk meesterschap en sociale intelligentie. Schiedam: Scriptum.
- Peters, T. (1982). In Search of Excellence. Lessons From America's Best-Run Companies. New York: Harper Collins.
- Pink, D. (2010). Drive. The Surprising Truth About What Motivates Us. New York: Riverhead Books.
- Prue, D. M. & Fairbank, J. A. (1981). Performance Feedback in Organizational Behavior Management A Review. Journal of Organizational Behavior Management, 3(1), 1-16.
- Rachman, S. (1989). Fear and Courage. New York: W.H. Freeman.
- Rheinberg, F., Manig, Y. & Kliegl, R. (2007). Flow bei der Arbeit, doch Glück in der Freizeit. Zeitschrift für Arbeits- und Organisationspsychologie, 51(3), 105-115.
- Rhenen, W. van (2008). From Stress to Engagement. Proefschrift Universiteit van Amsterdam. Geraadpleegd op http://dare.uva.nl/ document/107037.
- Rogatkho, T.P. (2009). The Influence of Flow on Positive Affect in College Students. Journal of Happiness Studies, 10(2), 133-148.

• Rothmann, S. & Storm, K. (2003). Work Engagement in the South African Police Service. Paper presented at the 11th European Congress of Work and Organizational Psychology, 14-17 mei 2003, Lissabon, Portugal.

• Salanova, M., Agut, S. & Peiró, J.M. (2005). Linking Organizational Resources and Work Engagement to Employee Performance and Customer Loyalty. The Mediating Role of Service Climate. Journal of Applied Psychology, 90, 1217-1227.

• Sarasvathy, S.D. (2001). Causation and Effectuation. Toward a Theoretical Shift From Economic Inevitability to Entrepreneurial Contingency. The Academy of Management Review, 26(2), 243-264.

• Schaper, F. (2003). Geen tijd voor burnout. Het verband tussen karakter, levensfase en stress.

• Schiedam: Scriptum.

• Schaufeli, W.B. & Bakker, A.B. (2001). Werk en welbevinden. Naar een positieve benadering in de Arbeids- en Gezondheidspsychologie. Gedrag & Organisatie, 14, 229-253.

• Schaufeli, W.B., Salanova, M., Gonzalez-Roma, V. & Bakker, A.B. (2002). The Measurement of Engagement and Burnout. A Two Sample Confirmatory Factor Analytic Approach. Journal of Happiness Studies, 3, 71-92.

• Schaufeli, W.B. & Bakker, A.B. (2004). Job Demands, Job Resources, and their Relationship with Burnout and Engagement. A Multi-Sample Study. Journal of Organizational Behavior, 25, 293-315.

• Schaufeli, W.B. & Taris, T.W. (2005). The Conceptualization and Measurement of Burnout. Common Ground and Worlds Apart. Work & Stress, 19(3), 256-262.

• Schaufeli, W.B., Taris, T.W. & Rhenen, W. van (2008). Workaholism, Burnout and Work Engagement. Three of a Kind or Three Different Kinds of Employee Well-Being? Applied Psychology: An International Review, 57, 173-203.

• Schwartz, T. (2012). The Magic of Doing One Thing at a Time. Geraadpleegd op http://blogs.hbr.org/2012/03/the-magic-of-doing-one-thing-a/.

• Seligman, M. & Csikszentmihalyi, M. (2000). Positive Psychology. An Introduction. American Psychologist, 55, 5-14.

• Sitter, L.U. de, Hertog, F. den & Dankbaar, B. (1997). From Complex Organizations with Simple Jobs to Simple Organizations with Complex Jobs. Human Relations, 30(5), 535-84.

• Sluis, L.E.C. van der (2008). Talent Management in strategisch perspectief. Breukelen: Nyenrode Business University.

• Sluis, L.E.C. van der & Berkhout, B. (2009). Nederland Talentenland. Themanummer Develop, 1, 1-7.

• Sluis, L.E.C. van der (2011). Interview Onderwijs & Communicatie. Geraadpleegd op http://onderwijs-communicatie.nl/2011/01/ 28/lidewey-van-der-sluis-over-talentmanagement-op-scholen/.

• Stoffelsen, J. & Diehl, P. (2007). Handboek levensfasebewust personeelsbeleid. Iedereen heeft recht op een verschillende aanpak. Alphen aan den Rijn: Kluwer.

• Taylor, F.W. (1911). The Principles of Scientific Management. New York, Londen: Harper & brothers.

• Tissen, R. (2008). Geef ze de ruimte! Schoonhoven: Academic Service.

• Verbraak, C. (2001). Joop van den Ende. 'De optelsom is: ik ben best een keurige man.' Vrij Nederland, 27 januari.

<u>References</u>

• Vleugel, R. (2011). Bevlogen werknemers
binnen organisaties: de rol van feedback bij het
faciliteren van workflow. Geraadpleegd op http://
www.academicrepublic.com/academicrepublic/
dissertations/5492_bevlogen_werknemers_binnen_
organisaties.pdf.
• Von Thiele Schwarz, U., Hasson, H. & Muntlin Athlin,
Å. (2011). Perceived Efficiency in the Emergency
Department. Low Throughput Rates or Having a Lot to
Do? Geraadpleegd op http://urn.kb.se/resolve?urn=urn:
nbn:se:uu:diva-170749.
• Welch, J. (2005). Winnen. Utrecht: Spectrum.
• Westman, M., Bakker, A.B., Roziner, I. & Sonnentag,
S. (2011). Crossover of Job Demands and Emotional
Exhaustion Within Teams. A Longitudinal Multilevel
Study. Anxiety, Stress & Coping, 24:5, 561-577. http://
dx.doi.org/10.1080/10615806.2011.558191.
• Winsemius, P. (2011). Je gaat het pas zien als je het
doorhebt. Over Cruijff en leiderschap. Amsterdam:
Uitgeverij Balans.
• Xanthopoulou, D., Bakker, A.B., Heuven, E., Demerouti,
E. & Schaufeli, W.B. (2008a). Working in the Sky. A
Diary Study Among Flight Attendants. Journal of
Occupational Health Psychology, 13, 345-356.
• Xanthopoulou, D., Bakker, A.B., Demerouti, E. &
Schaufeli, W.B. (2008b). How Job and Personal
Resources Influence Work Engagement and
Financial Returns. A Diary Study in a Greek Fast-Food
Company. Journal of Occupational and Organizational
Psychology, 82, 183-200.
• Zimbardo, P.G. (2010). Het Lucifer Effect.
Rotterdam: Lemniscaat.

Follow *Be a Hero* on Facebook:
www.facebook.com/sebastiaankodden

About the author

Bas Kodden is a writer, speaker and researcher in the field of leadership, entrepreneurship and personal development. The subject of engagement in particular.

🌐 www.baskodden.nl
🐦 @BasKodden
f wordeenheld
📷 sebastiaankodden
@ Bas@Kodden.net
📞 030-2611061

Also read the sequel to *Word een HELD: De Kunst van Duurzaam Presteren* (april 2017)

⭐⭐⭐⭐⭐ op Bol.com
⭐⭐⭐⭐⭐ op Managementboek.nl

'Read it open-mouthed'

'Amazing empirical research'

'Bas Kodden (again) has written a fantastic book'

And others: ManagementPro: 'A Must-Read'
Tijdschrift voor HRM: 'Highly recommended'

Volg *Word een HELD* op Facebook: www.facebook.com/wordeenheld